The Christian Counselor's Guide for Restoring Virginity

J.P. Sloane
Shannon Sloane

The Christian Counselor's Guide for Restoring Virginity

J.P. Sloane
Shannon Sloane

xulon PRESS

For more information or for speaking engagements, contact:
J. P. Sloane
Shannon Sloane
Angeles Crest Productions
2219 E. Thousand Oaks Boulevard
Thousand Oaks, CA 91362

https://www.jpsloane.com

www.xulonpress.com

Acknowledgments

We would like to thank God for enabling us to reason in love with those who are suffering in a sinful and fallen world through His own Divine revelation of Reason (or Logos), Jesus Christ.

We also wish to acknowledge all of the wonderful counselors and pastors who have dedicated themselves to serving their brothers and sisters in Christ. Thank you for availing yourselves of God's counsel through His Holy Word and, in the spirit of 2 Timothy 3:16, to guide and help your counselees in dealing with their troubled souls and sinful natures.

The Christian Counselor's Guide for Restoring Virginity

CONTENTS

INTRODUCTION

This *Christian Counselor's Guide for Restoring Virginity* is designed for biblical counselors who are tackling the counseling issue of restoring virginity. It is designed to stand on its own or to be used with our companion work book, *You Can Be a Virgin Again.* If you are using our counselees' parallel book in conjunction with your counseling program, you will find the two books to be reflective of each other (with appropriate modifications) which allows you, as a counselor, to understand exactly what the counselee is reading in the companion text. This book similarly approaches restored virginity, only from the counselor's perspective and gives additional insight for you as a counselor. In the Appendix of this book, we have supplied you with some data gathering forms which may be copied and enlarged for your counselee to complete. If your counselee is using our companion work book, these same forms have been included in the Appendix of their book to copy as well.

Through our counseling and interacting with people from all walks of life, two things became apparent: The frustration of counselees dealing with problems and not getting answers from the usual sources left them with a sense of hopelessness. Because their pastors tell them to seek "professional counseling," they are left wondering, "I thought pastors were professional ministers of the soul. Why do they send me out of the church for help that I thought the Bible should address?" More than once we heard, "If God made us, shouldn't He be able to give us the answers we need? If the Bible is God's Word, shouldn't we be able to find the answers to our problems and the answers to life in its pages?"

The second thing we heard is, "If only I had stayed a virgin, I wouldn't be pregnant now. If only I were still a virgin, I wouldn't have genital herpes" (or other sexually transmitted diseases). "If only I were still a virgin, I wouldn't be expected to sleep with every guy I went out with. If only I were still a virgin, I wouldn't have gotten my girlfriend pregnant and have to pay child support. If only I could be a virgin again, my mom and dad would be proud of me. If only I were still a virgin, I wouldn't have had to drop out of school. If only, if only ...."

As Christian counselors, we should know that the good news found in the Bible has all of the answers to these and other problems. Many people confess to us how unsatisfied they are with a noncommittal sex life which leaves them going from one sexual encounter to another and sometimes to the doctor as well! You may have had counselees who have been disillusioned over a recent affair complain, "If God made sex, it sure isn't all it's hyped up to be." They may have said this because they have experienced loneliness and betrayal many times. We developed this book so that Christian counselors may help people who are caught up in a never-ending cycle of affairs and disappointing hurts to drastically change their lives for the good. There is hope for restoring your counselees' virginity again as so many others have done!

Motivational speaker and author, Deborah Smith Pegues, cautions us how important God's word is, as well as the use of our own words when dealing with counselees:

> Words are our tools of communication. Words never die. They live on in the heart of the hearer. To maintain harmonious relationships in every facet of our (counselees) lives, we must learn to use words effectively. In His infinite wisdom, God has already equipped us to speak words that get the desired results: *"The Lord God hath given me the tongue of the learned that I should know how to speak a word in season to him that is weary"* (Isaiah 50:4).[1]

When researching our companion book, *You Can Be a Virgin Again,* we came across many people who were very encouraging to us regarding the need for such a book. On several occasions, we even had some parents ask us if that book would be good to give to their children who were just becoming aware of the physical changes occurring in their adolescent bodies. This inspired us to include: *Staying A Virgin Teen; Dealing With Feelings* (chapter 6) and *Staying A Virgin Teen; Guys Have Feelings Too* (chapter 7), which are aimed specifically toward your teenage counselees who are still virgins, but beginning to feel pressure from their friends, television, movies and even teachers at their schools who would advise them not to have sex until they are "mature enough to handle it." The problem with the latter advice, as you are aware, is that the Bible (and most civilized societies) never counseled their young people, or older people for that matter, not to have sex until they were "able to handle it." On the contrary, most religious groups and civilizations have always preferred that their societies would keep sex out of harm's way, which is done through the context of marriage. Of course, throughout history there have been morally corrupted societies. As Christian counselors, you are aware of those pagan societies that the early church, as well as the Jews, had to deal with in the Bible. Those societies became so corrupt that they were completely destroyed. Their destruction was usually a result of being focused on fleshly pleasures and evil pastimes; therefore, they began to crumble from within, which made it easier for their surrounding hostile countries to conquer them with relative ease!

This book is designed to be an encouraging biblically-based source that offers hope to those counselees who are seeking to restore their virtue and commit themselves to a lifestyle that honors God. The people referred to in our case histories are given fictitious names in an effort to protect them and any other person who coincidentally may have the same name.

We also deal with the ever-popular and omnipresent "good self-esteem" issue. It is unfortunate that not only the world, but the church as well, has bought into this psychological deception which we deal with in chapters one and seven. On the surface it appears like a good foundational concept. After all, no one likes to *feel* bad, and everyone loves to *feel* good about themselves; yet, what lies at the very heart of this axiom is the cleverly disguised promotion of the acceptance of a prideful heart. As we explain to your counselees in our companion book, self-esteem is a synonym for self-pride, and the Bible warns us that first we have pride (self-esteem) and then we have destruction (Proverbs 16:18; 1 Timothy 3:5). It would be wise for us to instruct our counselees that what they need is not good self-esteem, but good self-worth! Some may argue that they are both the same, but they are not. Esteem is self-focused while self-worth is a reflection of someone's value.

Reflect for a moment on the old story about a village where a bride was bought with a gift of livestock given to her father. If the daughter was from a highly respected family in the community, her price would be no less than a fine young bull or even a matched pair of oxen. However, if she was very pretty but from a poor family, her parents may be given several sheep; but if she was not so attractive, a goat would have to do. Now in this village lived the son of an average family who had fallen in love with a poor man's daughter who, on the surface, was not very pretty. Nevertheless, she had an inner beauty that drew this young man to her. He began working very hard to acquire enough wealth to purchase two fine oxen as the bridal payment for his intended bride. His friends thought he was foolish because he wanted to give such an extravagant gift to her father, but the young man would not be dissuaded. It took him almost two years longer than it would have if he had settled for a gift of a goat, but such was the price he wanted to pay. The big day came when the man proudly marched up to the door of the house of his intended wife to be. The whole village watched him march down the street accompanied with his friends and two of the most beautifully matched pair of oxen anyone had ever seen. How extravagant and costly this gift was! When the young man knocked on the door of his intended and asked her father for his daughter's hand in marriage, he presented the father with this most exceptional gift. The father was overcome and gladly rejoiced that his poor average daughter would become the wife of such a handsome and generous man! When the father called his daughter and showed her the wonderful bridal price the young man had offered for her, an amazing thing happened. Suddenly this average young girl's countenance began to change. The people of the village started murmuring among themselves, "Is this the same daughter of the poor old man? She seems somehow more gracious and lovely. She stands taller and there is a glow about her." After the wedding, the young wives began to admire her very much and gave her deference from that time on. She was a wonderful wife and treated her husband with exceptional love and respect because she was valued so highly by him. As Christians, we do not have a need for good self-esteem because we find our worth in Christ. While we were still sinners, Jesus valued us so much that He was willing to pay the ultimate price for us on Calvary's Cross (Romans 5:8). It is through His sacrifice and love that we find our self-worth, not through anything we did, but through everything He did for us! Therefore, only through Jesus is there any hope for your counselees to restore their virginity and restore it they can.

JESUS IS COMING FOR HIS BRIDE THE CHURCH AND
HE EXPECTS HER TO BE A VIRGIN!
2 Corinthians 11:2

NOTES:
1. Deborah Smith Pegues, *Managing Conflict God's Way* (New Kensington: Whitaker House, 1997), 89.

CHAPTER 1

RESTORED VIRGINITY

"With Man This Is Impossible; but With God All
Things Are Possible"

Jesus Christ

The world wants us to believe that once we lose our virginity, we have no hope of restoring our innocence. Your counselees may have bought into Satan's lie that they might just as well forget about their virtue and go with the times. After all, not being a virgin in today's society is very acceptable. The only ones they make fun of are virgins. If this is so, why are there so many divorces and pregnant women disappearing who later turn out to have been murdered, contracted the "heartbreak of herpes" and/or other venereal diseases? Many people who are living with their "significant others" (a popular term that has no biblical basis) wind up alone and broken-hearted over and over again. Many popular seeker-friendly churches offer divorce counseling and "group therapy" that act more as lonely hearts clubs to keep recycling "significant others," but after all, this is just considered normal today. If it is so normal, then why are there so many suffering and lonely people?

Nevertheless, more and more people have come to realize that the Bible and *old-fashioned family values* may offer a better alternative than the lifestyle the media and Hollywood are trying to sell us.

The truth is that our Creator God loves us so much that He only wants the best for us; but at the outset Satan entered our world, and the two basic lies that he used then are still being used against God's people today. The first lie is doubt (Genesis 3:1), which calls God's Word into question and suggests that God is a liar. The second is rejection (Genesis 3:4), which encourages a person to lose faith in God's Word and reject His teachings. Because of this, the moral principles that God laid out for us in order for us to have happy and meaningful lives, through godly relationships, has been perverted and have all but disappeared. God's Word never changes, and the truths He created in us from the beginning are still valid and still hold hope for us.

What we desire to help you show your counselees who are hurting and confused regarding their love and sexuality will become apparent through the chapters of this book. Once your counselees have had premarital sex, Satan will have them reasoning that they are no longer virgins, and they may as well "throw caution to the wind" and enjoy sex because they will never be a virgin again. This accusation destroys too many lives. The truth is that your counselees can restore their virginity and become a new person—a new creature in Christ!

We are not talking about people having a second virginity because that could lead to a third virginity, which could lead to a fourth virginity and so on. In time, they would become so callous about their failures and weak commitments to truly restoring their virginity that they could joke, "It's easy to become a virgin again. I do it all of the time between affairs!"

Counselees may be able to joke and make light of their problems with others, but the truth is that they are only fooling themselves. Because we live in a secular society, we are constantly being bombarded by glamorized sin. By definition, secularism is a worldly view without God; therefore, the pop-psychology programs we are constantly exposed to in our media are very misleading. Because secular psychology is by its very definition man-centered, it looks internally to man's thoughts and *feelings* for the answers. It teaches that everyone is basically good, but God teaches us, "… the heart of the sons (children) of men (humans) is full of evil, and madness is in their heart while they live …" (Ecclesiastes 9:3c, clarification ours). Allowing people to keep making mistakes because they "cannot help themselves" enables them to continue in a sinful and destructive lifestyle. Many secular psychologists say there is no such thing as sin. Sin is not politically correct, therefore, some secular psychologists tell us that we are all victims and are not supposed to be held accountable for our shortcomings. This sounds reasonable on the surface, but it leaves no hope for those who are suffering to believe that they will ever be capable of changing their lifestyles. The only hope we have of being set free is by acknowledging that we are in bondage to sin and cannot free ourselves.

If your counselees truly wish to alter and bring their desires under control, they cannot look to themselves for the answer, as some secular psychiatrists and secular psychologists would ask them to do, but they need to look for help from the One who created them—God. The truth is that we all need a Savior to save us from our bondage, and only through the knowledge and acceptance of such a Savior can we ever hope to escape from our problems. "And you shall know the truth and the truth shall make you free" (John 8:32). Since there is such a Savior, then it makes sense that we must seek Him and His will for our lives so He can help us.

Therefore, your counselees should not be seeking a second or a third virginity, but rather a *restored* virginity, a once and for all change in their lives that will allow them to truly become reborn— a new creation, fresh, wholesome—a virgin in thought, word and deed, as well as in fact.

They may ask, "How can this be possible?" Many of the young girls I talk with confidentially confess that if they could do it all over again, they would do things differently. I ask them, "Why not start over now?" The answer is always the same, "Because it's too late; I've already lost my virginity." They are really telling me that because they have already fallen into that lifestyle, they cannot stop.

No, it is not too late. There is a way out. Since we are talking about restored virginity, we must take a moment to define terms.

To begin with, what is a virgin? According to the *Random House Webster' College Dictionary*, a virgin is "a person who has never had sexual intercourse."[1] Tradition maintains that anyone who has had intimate touching of the sex organs is no longer considered a virgin. Virginity implies an innocence of carnal (fleshly) encounters. When someone marries a member of the opposite sex, it has been traditionally expected that neither spouse has been touched in any inappropriate place.[2] We see this concept in other subject areas as well. For instance, take the discoveries of exotic, far away places that no one has ever seen. To emphasize how pristine and unspoiled it is, the discovery of new terrain is often referred to as "virgin land" or "virgin wilderness."

The problem causing so much grief today is the lack of abstinence before marriage. What happened to confuse our national morality? Mixed messages bombard all of us today, suggesting we do one thing and then tell us to do something or else. Children are taught that there are no absolutes, meaning that everyone is allowed to make up his own definitions of right and wrong, which assails and corrupts any accurate definition of virginity. Most children used to look to the President of the United States of America as a role model. What is someone to think when one or more of the most influential people in the world redefines what has always been accepted as truth and distorts it for his own motives?

In one recent sad footnote to history, the United States had a president who was exposed for having an extramarital affair. His defense was that he only had "oral sex" and he said that was not considered "sexual relations." For months, all we heard was that oral sex is not really sex. By its own definition, it was sex. The president's defenders protested that the dictionary does not describe oral sex as "sex," so the president was innocent of the charge of having "sexual relations." The president himself shook his finger at the television camera while insisting that he "... did not have 'sexual relations' with that woman ...." Pausing, he pretended that he had forgotten her name until after a dramatic brief moment as if it was an afterthought, he remembered it. I wonder how many other women have just as easily been forgotten when their boyfriends are caught by their "significant other" woman or wife.

The problem with the president's comment claiming that oral sex was not defined in any dictionary to be sexual relations is that it was repeated and heard many times (the press kept replaying it) by many teenagers. After awhile, they began to believe it, and even worse, they began to practice it!

How does the dictionary define the term sexual relations? *Random House Webster's College Dictionary* states that sexual relations is "1. sexual intercourse; coitus. 2. any sexual activity between individuals."[3] Notice the second definition for sexual relations states that *any* sexual activity, and oral sex is a sexual activity!

We have all of this nitpicking because there has been a reinvention of how our nation views traditionally-held beliefs by redefining and misdirecting our moral compass.

This is reflected in an encounter that the award-winning author, Eleanor Ayer, had with a young married couple. She tells of how a girl wanted to please her boyfriend, but she always put an end to their "fooling around" before intercourse occurred. Her boyfriend loved her, but he wanted to have sex. He finally convinced her that if he pulled out before he had a climax and if she did not reach one either, she would still be able to keep her commitment of abstinence.[4]

Ayer is not the only one who has had some interesting counselees. In my own counseling, I have heard some incredible excuses. One young girl was convinced that since she only submitted herself to anal sex (sodomy), she was still a virgin because her hymen was not broken. This is self-deception. When people want to sin but their conscience bothers them, they seek to find a loophole to allow themselves to continue in a sinful lifestyle while pretending to still practice abstinence. Purity is not indicated by a woman possessing a hymen anymore than holiness is indicated by a male who is circumcised. Paul says in Romans 2:28-29, "For he is not a Jew, which is one outwardly; neither is that circumcision, which is outward in the flesh: But He is a Jew, which is one inwardly; and circumcision is that of the heart, in the spirit, and not in the letter; whose praise is not of men, but of God." In God's eyes, purity is determined by the heart.

Just because your counselee is no longer physically a virgin does not mean she is ruined or that there is no hope for her. However, before your counselee can have any hope of restoring herself, she must address the problem for what it is. The activities she has been engaged in are not a right of passage but an entanglement of sin. That is not a word we hear much in our society, and we can see the results in the behavior of our neighbors and ourselves. Once we acknowledge that sin is at the root of our problem, through the Bible we are able to address that sin and get rid of it. Sinful indiscretions happen to everybody, but as biblical counselors we know people can and do change with the help of God. They can begin a new life with their virginity restored to them. "Therefore, if any (hu)man be in Christ, (s)he is a new creature: old things are passed away; behold, all things are become new ..." (2 Corinthians 5:17, clarification ours). Spiritually, sin is eradicated because we are born-again; we no longer need to look at our fellow humans and their circumstances in the same way (2 Corinthians 5:16), nor do we regard Christ in the same way. In verse 18, God does not look at us in the same way either because our spirit is without sin, but our flesh still wars against us. Matthew 26:41 states, "Watch and pray, that you enter not into temptation: the spirit is willing, but the flesh is weak."

Being born-again carries the responsibility of understanding just what it means to be born-again. In today's society, the government's public schools have programmed us to think of ourselves as owing no allegiance to anyone other than ourselves. Students are continually instructed that their bodies are their own and, therefore, they can do whatever they wish with them. However, in order to be born-again, we have to understand that a price was paid for our salvation and that we no longer belong to ourselves but to our Savior, Christ. We must realize that once we are born-again, our bodies become extensions of Christ.

Who would take a member of Christ and join it to someone who has been sexually immoral and sleeping around? God forbid! We need to realize that when we join ourselves sexually to another person, we become one flesh. However, when we are joined unto the Lord, we become one spirit. It is profitable to flee fornication. Every sin we commit is outside the body, but when we have sexual relationships outside of marriage, we sin against our own body. We must realize that our bodies are the temple of the Holy Spirit, which is now in every believer. Therefore, when we become born-again, our bodies become the temple of God and are no longer ours to do with what we wish (1 Corinthians 6:15-19, clarification ours).

Then it is no wonder when counselees first begin to have sexual encounters outside of marriage that they feel conflicted. On one hand, the desire for intimate relations is very strong and satisfying. On the other hand, something or someone (i.e., the Holy Spirit) tells us that what we are doing is not right. Some people call this inner voice their conscience, but the truth is that we feel this twinge of guilt because we know we are going against the best that God has for us. Sometimes in a moment of passion, that little voice is drowned out. As your counselees become very promiscuous, they cease to hear it altogether. Sooner or later, their lives are filled with regret. Once they understand that their regret is a manifestation of a sinful life, and they realize that they have lived a life of rebellion against God's best for them, they stand at a crossroads.

The first reaction is as follows: Many females (this could apply to males as well) have told me that once they have had sex they believe there is no turning back, and God would never forgive them. They usually continue in abusive relationships for the rest of their lives. Of course, it is easy for us who are standing on the outside to be judgmental, but the truth is that when these girls listen to the lies of Satan, they believe that their sin is larger than God's ability to forgive them. Once they have had sexual relationships, they believe it is impossible to ever attain a state of grace again. The problem with this is that they are basing their relationship with God and their salvation on their works. Fortunately, Paul assures us, "For by grace are you saved through faith; and that not of yourselves: it is the gift of God: not of works, lest any man should boast" (Ephesians 2:8-9). We are saved by grace. Grace is a word not many people understand. It simply means that something has been given to us that we do not deserve, but nonetheless are able to have.

The second reaction is when your counselee listens to that voice that has been nagging her and she realizes her life must change. Your counselee is finally acknowledging that the guilt conviction she has been trying to avoid is actually God's concern for her life. She is really experiencing the Holy Spirit who only wants God's best for her. It is at this crossroads when your counselee turns to the other path because she realizes that she has made poor choices that have led her into a state of sin, acknowledges that sin, and makes a decision that she no longer wants to go down a path of destruction. To turn away from sin and seek another direction (the path of righteousness) is called repentance. It is through repentance and the acknowledgement that she has sinned, and no longer want to continue in that sin, that she is now able to receive God's forgiveness and help.[5]

It is important at this point for your counselee to stop and understand that when we repent and make a decision to *stop* sinning, our feelings and simple desires will not just evaporate and leave us alone. The exciting news is we have divine help to overcome temptation! Will Satan leave us alone because we have committed ourselves to God? Hardly. He tempted Jesus (who is God Himself), but because Jesus did not give into temptation, we can depend on Him to help us struggle against that which is trying to destroy us. Will we stumble? Of course we might; but there is a difference between stumbling through some unforeseen event and deliberately planning to sin and ask forgiveness later. It is a question of commitment and the attitude of our heart.

God created us with the free will to choose, and He will not force us to do anything that we do not wish to do. It is our choice. However, if your counselees want God's help, He will help them overcome their sinful lifestyle and restore their virginity because, "There is no temptation taken you but such as is common to (a hu)man: but God is faithful, who will not suffer (allow) you to be tempted above that (which) you are able; but will with the temptation also make a way of escape, that you may be able to bear it ..." (1 Corinthians 10:13, clarification ours). However, without Christ, there is no hope (Ephesians 2:12).

One of the greatest lies of the world is that we must hold ourselves in high esteem, and that we must somehow *feel* good about ourselves no matter what we do in order to function as a normal human being. This concept comes from modern secular psychology which in and of itself is an oxymoron. Consider this: The founders of modern secular psychology were all atheists and agnostics; yet, they are telling us how we should perceive the study of the soul (i.e., psychology). For humans to function and have any worth, we must realize that we are sinful by nature. In fact, the Bible states, "... the heart of the sons of men is full of evil, and madness is in their hearts while they live ..." (Ecclesiastes 9:3). We are also warned, "The heart is deceitful above all things, and desperately wicked: who can know it" (Jeremiah 17:9)? Our worth is far more than just the approval of our fellow human creatures. The truth is that the living God took our form and allowed Himself to be cruelly demeaned, beaten and murdered in order to pay a price no one else would or could pay for our depraved nature. As for high self-esteem, the world wants us to believe that if we do not think highly of ourselves, we must then think of ourselves as inferior and act accordingly. However, God says we are to, "Let nothing be done through strife or vainglory, but in lowliness of mind let each esteem others better than ourselves" (Philippians 2:3). *Webster's College Dictionary* defines esteem as "to regard highly or favorably, to regard with respect or admiration."[6] When we hold ourselves in high esteem, we are showing the sin of pride (Psalm 59:12). If we think highly of ourselves and want to *feel* good about ourselves, the resulting failure in our character would be the desire to have sexual liaisons that boost our ego and create a momentary sense of well-being and desirability. However, this behavior is considered sin (fornication) in God's eyes. Think about this for a moment: The Bible warns us of many terrible things that will be seen in the last days before Armageddon, and the very first evil thing on that list is that "people will be lovers of themselves." In other words, people will possess a high self-esteem. "This know also, that in the last days perilous times shall come. For men shall be *lovers of their own selves*, covetous, boasters, proud, blasphemers, disobedient to parents, unthankful, unholy ..." (2 Timothy 3:1-2, clarification ours). I had always wondered how such a thing could happen, but now it seems obvious. This is brought about through secular psychology, which keeps insisting that we must have good self-esteem, or we cannot function properly. This kind of thinking is just plain wrong. All of us desire to be confident; none of us desire to be despondent. We do not like to be depressed about ourselves and our lives; but we should not be taken in by so-called self-esteem. It is only through God that our inner need for love and self-acceptance is met. It is God's love for us that enables us to love others properly and find our own true *worth* and *value*.

Before we discover how counselees can restore their virginity, we will take a look in the following chapters at the real world where we find ourselves living, as well as some of the real temptations and trials with which we are confronted daily.

NOTES:
1. *Random House Webster's College Dictionary* (1990), s.v. "virgin."
2. Elisabeth Elliot, *Passion and Purity: Learning to Bring Your Love Under Christ's Control* (Grand Rapids: Fleming H. Revell, 1984), 20. Elliot expresses how women traditionally realized how precious their virginity was. It was a protected treasure that she guarded for the man who would be willing to pay for it, and that payment was in the form of a marital commitment exclusively to her.
3. *Random House Webster's College Dictionary* (1990), s.v. "sexual relations."
4. Eleanor Ayer, *It's Okay to Say No: Choosing Sexual Abstinence* (New York: The Rosen Publishing Group, Inc., 1977), 25.
5. Jay E. Adams, *A Theology of Christian Counseling—More Than Redemption* (Grand Rapids: Zondervan Publishing House, 1979), 197. Adams suggests the motivating force that directs us toward repentance is a feeling of guilt.
6. *Random House Webster's College Dictionary*, (1990), "esteem."

CHAPTER 2

JUST A MATERIAL GIRL
LIVING IN A MATERIAL WORLD

At the dawn of the twenty-first century, we live in a world where distance is no longer a barrier. When we sit in our homes or offices and call a company for technical assistance on its product, we might find ourselves speaking to someone in India, the Philippines or some other exotic place! With the click of a computer mouse, we are able to access the Internet, which is an instant information highway to countries around the world. We can be sitting in Los Angeles and read the London Times that originates in the United Kingdom. With another click, the Jerusalem Post is accessible with the latest news about Israel. Knowledge abounds, but Christians seem to be as ill-informed about their faith as they were centuries ago.

What does this have to do with virtue?[1] In our world, the media is inescapable. Televisions, radios, movies, ads on the Internet, ads on highway billboards—all promoting lust for things, status and sex. Eleanor Ayer points out how sex is used on television to sell products and programming. She states that in a typical 60 minute show, on an average there are three sexual acts (soap operas are even higher, showing 1,500 acts of sex yearly). Sexual trysts between unmarried couples are shown six times as much, as compared to married couples. Teenagers learn how to dress and act by watching what is presented on television. Peer pressure and friends, combined with portrayed lifestyles in the media, pressure young people to pursue and engage in sex even when they have no desire. In Georgia, a study was done in Atlanta that reveals 90% of girls 15 and under want to learn to say no to sex. Ayer continues to reflect that traditionally, people have waited for marriage before they engaged in sex. It is her observation that some teens are slowly returning to that commitment in spite of all of the pressures they face.[2] The Associated Press reports a study that shows one of the pressures teens face is sexually explicit music because it encourages teens to engage in early sexual relationships. The report shows that debasing sexual lyrics influences teens to sexually act them out. The article reports that the songs portray guys as "sex-driven studs" and girls as objects of sex, complete with descriptive sex acts depicted that seem to stimulate the playing out of actual sex acts in younger and younger kids. However, in songs where relationships are less sexually described and presented in a more traditional way, the affect produced less sexual pressure among those young people who preferred that kind of music, resulting in more committed and moral relationships. The report states, "Teens who listened to lots of music containing sexually degrading messages became twice as likely to begin engaging in sexual behavior within two years after they started listening to such music as opposed to teens who only listened to very little or no sexually demeaning music." The article states that the study was conducted through 1,461 phone interviews of children between the ages of 12 and 17 years of age. The participants were virgins when first questioned and the statistics were gathered over a two-year period in order to find out what affect, if any, this genre of music had on them. The study appears in the August, 2006 issue of *Pediatrics*.[3] It is very important for your counselees to take responsibility and guard what they allow to enter through the gates of their eyes and ears.

In the early twentieth century, the world was less accessible. Radios were harmless because of the moral content and family-based audience. With the advent of television, controls (moral oversight boards) were in place to assure that the sensitivities of a moral nation would not be abused. Freedom of speech has come to mean a license to say or do anything our imagination can conjure up. Even within orthodoxy, we see some Episcopal churches, some Methodist churches, the Presbyterian Church USA, and others approving of sexual acts that are specifically forbidden in the Word of God. All of this is to justify the church as somehow being *modern* and up-to-date in a *sophisticated* world, and by today's standards, the church evidently does not want to appear *old-fashioned* and not hip.

This should not surprise us since Paul writes in 2 Timothy 4:3-4, "For the time will come when they will not endure sound doctrine; but after their own lusts shall they heap to themselves teachers, having itching ears (apostate religious leaders who tell them what they *want* to hear); And they shall turn away their ears from the truth, and (their religious beliefs) shall be turned unto fables" (clarification ours). We see people who want to continue in certain sexual lifestyles as well as other lifestyles that are opposed by the Bible. So-called "Christian" clergy approve of contrary biblical lifestyles by reading into Scripture something that is not there in order to justify immoral behaviors—behaviors that the Bible calls sin.

Having said this, most counselees' knowledge of the Bible is so vague that they cannot even list or recite seven of the Ten Commandments. As Christians, we do not look at the Ten Commandments as oppressive laws to spoil our fun, but rather we look to them as a road map for a safe journey through life. Unfortunately, for some who identify themselves as "church-going Christians," it is the atmosphere, the facility and the right type of music that influences them to frequent a particular church. Regrettably, as long as the pastor is not a boring speaker and is a charismatic figure, they are drawn to him rather than to Christ and His conviction. This is not to say that a charismatic preacher is necessarily a bad thing. There are many wonderful charismatic preachers of the gospel such as Billy Graham, Franklin Graham, Bishop Charles E. Blake and Jack Hayford who, while differing on denominational points, still manage to teach solid salvation issues.

What is the difference between someone like Billy Graham and Sun Young Moon (self-proclaimed Christ and spiritual leader of the Moonies)? The difference is in the message. When we deviate from Scripture, everything becomes permissible. Unfortunately, because of the spiritual ignorance of the average Christian, the world sees no difference in our lifestyles and those of pagans or hedonistic heathens. A hedonist is someone who seeks pleasure and sexual gratification while heathens do not acknowledge the God of the Bible.

The reason we are elaborating so much on this is because of the appalling statistics of immorality that we now find, to our shame, in the church. At the beginning of the twenty-first century, evangelical Christians have a higher rate of divorce than non-Chrisians.[4]

Among the girls I counseled, the rate of premarital sex and abortion was just as high among Christian teenagers as it was among non-Christians. When talking with pregnant, unwed mothers, it is not uncommon for them to tell me that it is alright for them to have an abortion and be a Christian because God will forgive them. These young ladies have pulled out of Scripture (or what they think they have heard about Scripture) the thought of forgiveness with no accountability, which makes them feel good about their sin. No one has pointed out to them Galatians 6:7: "Do not be deceived, God is not mocked; for whatever a man sows this he will also reap." Probably the most poignant message is in the following verse: "For the one who sows to his own flesh will from the flesh reap corruption" (Galatians 6:8a). We see in this passage that we cannot "con" God. He is not some gray-haired, feeble-minded old man looking down and doting on His children who, in His eyes, can do no wrong. The fact is that we are hard pressed to do right in God's eyes. We are not saying that God is a harsh deity who desires to make life as miserable as He can for us. "God so loved the world that He sent His only begotten Son so that whosoever believes in Him shall not perish but have everlasting life" (John 3:16), and this includes your counselee. If Abraham was willing to offer up His son, Isaac, for God, how much more was it for God to offer up His Son, Jesus, for us? God saved us not because of anything we have done, but because of the life, death and resurrection of our Lord, Jesus Christ.

So, while it is true that "We are saved by grace and not of works lest any man should boast," (Ephesians 2:8-9), we cannot take God for granted. Some individuals I have counseled offered the following in their defense: "Okay, so I made a mistake and I'm sorry. Anyway, God will forgive me." They then suggested that because they sinned, God will forgive them even more if they decide to have an abortion. The problem with this thinking is the belief that a person can do whatever they choose without fearing any reprisal from God because, "After all," they might say, "I've been baptized, so I'm saved and I'm going to heaven anyway." Paul warns us that this type of thinking is extremely dangerous when he states, "For the wrath of God is revealed from heaven against all ungodliness and unrighteousness of men, who hold the truth in unrighteousness" (Romans 1:18).

Again, this is the attitude that many in the church take away with them from the *feel good* theology. However, what Paul says is not being taught from the pulpit when he addresses this same type of belief, "What shall we say then? Shall we continue in sin, that grace may abound? God forbid" (Romans 6:1-2a).

It is important for your counselees who claim to be Bible-believing Christians not to assume that they have a permissive Father who winks at their indiscretions and turns a blind eye when they sin because they claim Jesus as their Lord. Jesus says, "Think not that I am come to destroy the law, or the prophets: I am come not to destroy, but to fulfill" (Matthew 5:17).

So how do your counselees reconcile Paul's teaching when he states, "For sin shall not have dominion over you; for you are not under the Law, but under grace" (Romans 6:14). Is God sending us mixed messages? Not at all. Let us suppose for a moment that the earth is made up of snakes and lambs and that God gave two commandments to this world stating, "Thou shalt not inject venom into another," and "Thou shalt not constrict the life out of your fellow creatures." Consider that God sends *His Lamb* into this world, and those who will receive Him will be born-again into the family of lambs. The "two commandments" are still valid, but the serpents who were born-again and no longer look or acted as serpents because they became lambs are no longer under the law. Consider a lamb. It does not have fangs to inject venom, nor the desire to do so because he has a different makeup. As for the second commandment, it is not the lamb's nature to squeeze something to death. A serpent, on the other hand, by its very nature strikes out, grabs and constricts the other creatures. So, while the lamb lives in a world where the law is still in effect, the law does not apply to him. The snake, who has become a lamb, is not troubled or tempted to strike or constrict anymore because he has the nature of the Lamb of God, and it is no longer in its nature to do such things. (In chapter 8 we approach this concept with the men from a different perspective and in more detail.)

Therefore, if we truly accept Christ as our Savior, and the desire of our heart is to be like Jesus and if we are like Jesus, the attraction to sin will begin to fade. When we are in Christ, the desires of our old nature become less attractive to us while the desire to be like Christ becomes more appealing, not because of laws but because of love. We are law-abiding, not because we have to be, but because we want to be; consequently, we strive to be more and more like Christ out of love rather than out of fear. Dr. Peter Marshall expressed it in a very simple and profound way when he said, "Freedom is not to do what we please but the freedom to do what is right."[5]

Unfortunately, what we have seen in our dealings with hundreds of girls and guys who have lost their virginity and claim to be Christians is an incredible ignorance, not only of the Word of God, but of the Spirit of the Scriptures as well. We cannot only keep what we agree with in Scripture and discard the rest. That would be like buying a new automobile and choosing to pay only for the two tires on the right, or on the curb-facing side of the car, because those are the only tires a passenger or pedestrian will see. As nice as that car may look from that viewpoint, it is not going to go anywhere without the other two tires on the driver's side.

One of the most heartbreaking things I hear from girls is that once they realize they have bought into the deception of the world, they cannot go back and undo sexual relations once they have taken place; and they definitely cannot bring back to life the child who was aborted from the womb. It is not as gloomy an outlook as some of the girls I have counseled first thought. If the girl is truly sorry for having engaged in premarital sex and has repented before God in her heart, perhaps restoring her virginity might not be as impossible as she first may think, and God will forgive her for having the abortion.

However, while the desired effect is the restoration of virginity, we must not lose sight that the desire to restore virginity is not the end in itself, but is the result of a problem that goes much deeper.

In order to permanently restore someone's virginity, be it male or female, it is imperative that we line ourselves up in a direct and positive relationship with the One God who designed us and our sexuality in the first place.[6]

Only through a right relationship with God can the hope of restoration of a permanent nature be realized. Therefore, the focus should be on attaining harmony with what God desires for our lives and a personal relationship with Christ. All other problems, including sexuality, then become manageable.

Modern secular psychology is a man-centered discipline. The Bible is God-centered. Therefore, when counselees take the advice of modern secular psychologists who tell them to *feel* good about themselves, they are basing their whole world-view on *feelings* rather than on *fact*. If we trust *feelings* regarding forgiveness, we may continue along life's road continually being offensive, destructive, hateful, and immoral because all we have to do is forgive ourselves. Forgiving ourselves has no lasting value. Counselees must also truly repent of their sinful activity. Forgiveness can be played out over and over again. True repentance is a one time commitment (1 John 1:8-10). Many people go wrong by continuing to believe, "Oh, I can forgive myself" or "God will forgive me again." However, this by its very presupposition sets us up for failure. Repentance is a commitment that we will never commit a sin again. Trusting in an endless chain of forgiveness for the same sin is not only mocking ourselves but God too. Your counselees can be assured that God is forgiving, but He is not some doting and permissive old fool who looks the other way when we disobey Him.

When we build upon our *feelings* and self-acceptance, we are constructing an edifice built upon sand that will eventually crumble. When we look at ourselves through God's eyes rather than through our own eyes, we are able to see our weaknesses and develop a godly structure that can stand against the destructive elements of our society. When we construct a positive goal for our lives that is built upon God's Word, we are building a solid foundation that has proven itself to last throughout history. When the winds of change try to destroy our current social fabric, the Bible makes it possible for us to withstand the evil fickleness of morality that the world tries to thrust upon us. Counseling offices are filled with well-meaning people who keep forgiving themselves over and over again but they return to square one asking, "What's wrong? Why can't I be happy? Why do I keep failing?" The answer is that by believing in yourself, you are believing in a very inept god.

It is important to remember that one of the reasons your counselees want to restore their virginity is because of the feeling of guilt. People instinctively know (who is the Holy Spirit) when they do something wrong. Someone inside of your counselees is telling them that they have made an improper decision, a wrong choice or behavior that is not acceptable. One may argue, "Who is to say what is right or wrong, and by what standard do we judge? To say you have an exclusive truth is bigoted." All we have to do is stand back and look at the different sections of our society who proclaim these types of arguments. Many of them are rebellious, and their dress and attitudes are confrontational. Divorce, children without fathers and abortion are not uncommon. Suicide and murder are prevalent and in general, they live a life of chaos and helplessness.

On the other hand, when we observe Christians who strive to live their lives to please God, not because they are afraid of His wrath, but because His love motivates them, we see an entirely different type of lifestyle. This does not mean that there are not difficulties and tragedies in the lives of Christians. However, their ability to cope and survive in a much more positive and beneficial way can be observed by others. So many times we have seen committed Christians who have undergone some of life's challenges being asked by their friends, "How do you do it? You've gone through so much, but you still have hope. I wish I had what you have." This is not an accident. In a world of hopelessness where we have been taught that we have evolved from some slime pit and are nothing more than an accident of the animal kingdom, life offers only hopelessness and death. On the other hand, Christians are survivors. They know they are special in the cosmos because they understand God has known them from the beginning of time, and He has plans for their lives (Romans 8:29). Therefore, your counselees can celebrate their virginity not to please man but to glorify God.

Consider the Ten Commandments (Exodus 20). If everyone practiced a lifestyle that corresponds with the directions God gives us in those commandments, this would be a better world. Think about it! You could leave your brand new flashy sports car sitting in the parking lot with the keys in it, and it would be there when you came back. Imagine losing your wallet in another part of town and someone chasing after you to return it. What an incredible world this would be! Your counselee as a child, no matter what her age, would never fight with her parents. For counselees with children, have them consider what it would be like for them to never be hurt or disappointed by their kids because their children *are* trustworthy. God has a plan for your counselees' lives, and He is not a spoil sport. He wants your counselees to enjoy life and enjoy it to its fullest. Sex is so incredible because God designed the mechanisms that make it function in such a way as to give great pleasure. Pleasure to be shared between a man and a woman is a tremendous bond which, during the act, literally unites a couple as one. However, misusing this gift as God originally intended it to be used is to open ourselves up to suffering, sorrow and even death.

Some research has been done on human bonding which shows that we have a hormone known as *oxytocin*, a neuro-peptide designed by God that acts as reinforcement for forming permanent family attachments. When a mother has given birth and begins nursing her baby, *oxytocin* begins a chemical reaction in her body which reinforces her "attachment" or bonding to her new baby. This is one of the reasons why a mother has strong bonds to her children.

Likewise, when a woman has a sexual relation, this same *oxytocin* comes into play. Each time she has sex, this hormone reinforces her commitment to the man with whom she is sexually active. However, if she has more than one partner, the affect of *oxytocin* begins to be produced in lower levels, and thus results in limiting her ability to bond. Having sex with multiple partners results in weakening the woman's ability to commit to one person. It can inhibit the kind of bond that God intended to exist between a wife and her husband, putting her future marriage in jeopardy. Researchers Dr. Diggs and Dr. Keroac warn, "People who have misused their sexual faculty and become bonded to multiple persons will diminish the power of oxytocin to maintain a permanent bond with an individual."[7]

In his book, *If You Really Loved Me*, Jason Evert puts it this way: "In more basic terms, sharing the gift of sex is like putting a piece of tape on another person's arm. The first bond is strong, and it hurts to remove it. Shift the tape to another person's arm and the bond will still work, but it will be easier to remove. Each time this is done, part of each person remains with the tape. Soon it is easy to remove because the residue from the various arms interferes with the tape's ability to stick. The same is true in relationships, where previous sexual experiences interfere with the ability to bond."[8]

Even males have the *oxytocin* hormone, but because the female hormone estrogen augments the affect of the *oxytocin*, the affect on males is less. This may explain why men do not bond as strongly as women at first when having sex. This is not to say that *oxytocin* does not have some of the same long-term positive effects on virgin men who wait until marriage to sexually bond with their wives. It seems that within the context of a virgin marriage, the *oxytocin* heightens the sexual stimulation. Therefore, when virgins marry, not only will the sexual relationship be especially gratifying, it will have a greater longevity throughout the marriage relationship as opposed to those who sleep around with multiple partners![9] However, as interesting as this is, remember it is not all physical; there is a spiritual component as well.

God's purpose for our lives and happiness is perfect. It is only when we allow ourselves to do things outside of God's will that we suffer the consequences. When the Bible was given to us, no one knew about hormones and how complicated they were. Only recently have scientists discovered them and how they work and interact with the human body. Of course, God understands His complex human design and in order to protect us, He gives us simple rules on how to conduct our lives so we may live them to the fullest. Caution your counselees not to do something that for the moment seems romantic and wonderful and cheat themselves out of the real meaningful bonding between them and their future spouse and family. They would be taking the chance that loosing their virginity may be alright because "everybody is doing it" or because he wants you to "prove your love for him." Sex is wonderful, but your counselees will only cheat themselves out of God's best for their lives if they do.

We only have to look at a newspaper advice column written by *Dear Abby* to see the consequences of misusing this gift as God originally intended it to be used by engaging in premarital sex.[10] In this article, we have several people responding to the previous article of a 14-year-old teenage girl who thinks that because all of her friends are having sex, she should join in the activity too. Several other girls who have been in her situation or a similar one, write to warn her that it is a big mistake based upon their unhappy experiences. One girl relates that she gave herself to a boy she loved and she thought he loved her, only to find out later that he only wanted to *score* with a virgin. He is gone and all of his friends have tried to *score* with her too. Her reputation was ruined, and that first experience left her with *ten* sexual affairs in just four years. That is an average of a new sex partner about every four months. Sadly, the article implies that sex outside of marriage that the Bible acknowledges as fornication is okay if you wait until you are older but is it? Please study the chart at the end of this chapter and see for yourself just how dangerous having multiple sexual partners outside of marriage really is, and keep in mind that the young girl we just read about had *ten* sexual partners in only four years. According to the chart at the end of this chapter, how many sexual partners did she *really* have? How many chances does she have of contacting a devastating sexually transmitted disease, many of which are incurable, and what is the likelihood that she may be harboring or be a carrier for sexually transmitted diseases in her body now and not even know about it? Waiting for sex outside of marriage until you are older leaves you just as vulnerable whether you are 14, 50 or any age. Without a commitment of marriage, you can easily be *dumped* regardless of how old you are.

Your counselees need to understand that virginity is also a sexual gift. It is a one-time present to be shared with the one person God has ordained for them to share their lives. Why should your counselees spoil that gift by abusing it with those who do not appreciate your counselee as much as they crave that moment of gratification?

The good news is that by aligning themselves with God's purpose for their lives, your counselees can have a permanent restoration of their virginity because now they should realize it is not a momentary toy to be played with and then cast aside; rather, it is a gift from God that is special and holy. Toys are pulled out of the closet to satisfy our whims and tossed aside when we lose interest, but a gift of great value is held in high esteem, protected, cherished and placed in a secure place of honor.

Jesus teaches us, "With God all things are possible ..." (Matthew 19:26b). Before we ask God for something foolish, we must remember that God is sovereign and does His own will, not every whim that we ask of Him. However, if we ask God for something in accordance with His will, He will hear us. If we know that He hears us, we know that He will answer us (1 John 5:14-15). God would certainly approve of your counselee's desire to become a virgin again.

In the following chapters, we will realistically look at the pressures your counselees face in today's world. We will see examples of propaganda by "learned people" and their advice for the "new morality." We will also see the inconsistency of some of these people when held up to the measuring stick of reality. The Alan Guttmacher Institute has inadvertently given some of the best ammunition against premarital sex. In the following chapters, we will also see that there is hope not just for women, but for men as well, to restore their virtue and virginity.

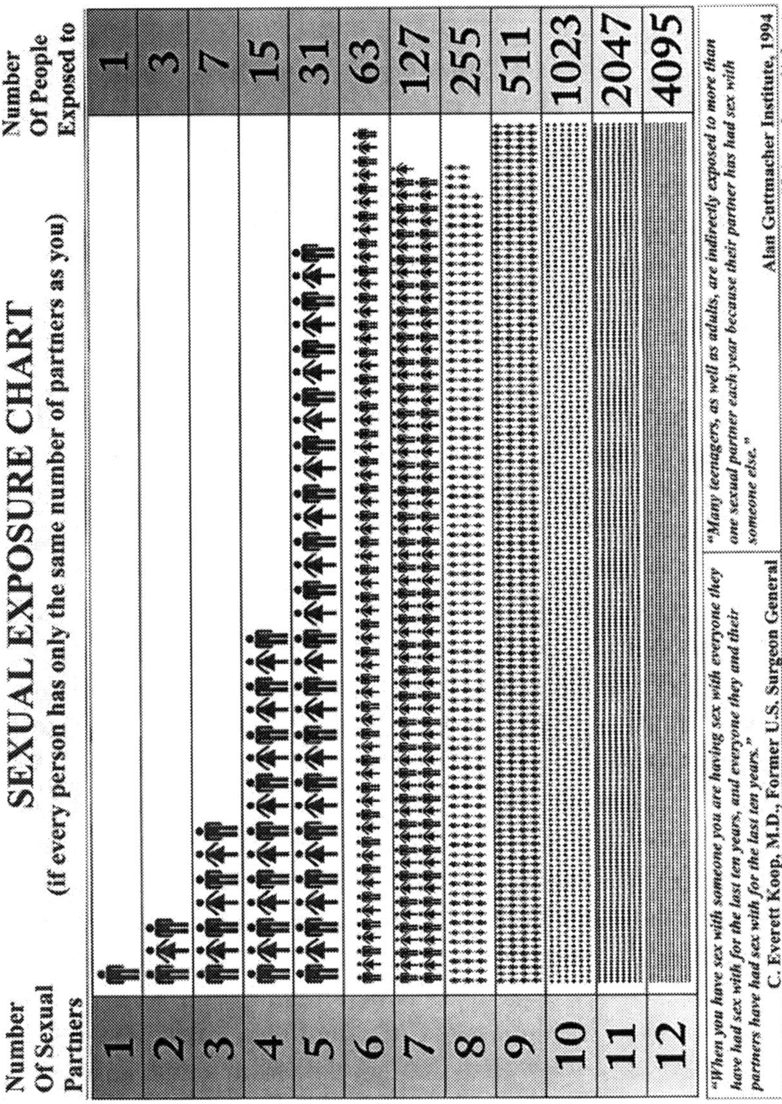

SEXUAL EXPOSURE CHART

(if every person has only the same number of partners as you)

Number Of Sexual Partners		Number Of People Exposed to
1		1
2		3
3		7
4		15
5		31
6		63
7		127
8		255
9		511
10		1023
11		2047
12		4095

"When you have sex with someone you are having sex with everyone they have had sex with for the last ten years, and everyone they and their partners have had sex with for the last ten years."
C. Everett Koop, M.D., Former U.S. Surgeon General

"Many teenagers, as well as adults, are indirectly exposed to more than one sexual partner each year because their partner has had sex with someone else."
Alan Guttmacher Institute, 1994

This chart used by permission of *Why kNOw Abstinence Programs*, Chattanooga, TN, and was modified to conform to this format.

Fig. 1

NOTES:
1. David F. Wells, *Losing Our Virtue* (Grand Rapids: William B. Eerdmans Publishing Company, 1998), 58. According to researchers Peter Kim and James Patterson, we are uniquely compared to any past generation because we no longer depend upon great moral leaders and the foundations of the Bible from which they drew their strength. We are adrift without a compass. We no longer have any objective reasoning, and divine moral absolutes have been reduced to myths.
2. Eleanor Ayer, *It's Okay to Say No: Choosing Sexual Abstinence* (New York: The Rosen Publishing Group, Inc., 1977), 15-16.
3. Associated Press, "Dirty song lyrics can prompt early teen sex. Degrading messages influence sexual behavior, study finds." http://msnbc.msn.com/id/14227775/?GT1=8404 (7 August, 2006).
4. Kerby Anderson, B.S., M.A., M.F.S., http://www.probe.org/docs/c-divorce.html. "Kerby Anderson's Commentaries," January 12, 2000. Anderson states that one out of every four people in the United States has had at least once divorce. The divorce rate of born-again Christians is even higher than non-Christians. George Barna, *The Future of America* (Chicago: Moody Press, 1993), 70. As of 1993, studies showed that the denominations who looked upon divorce as unacceptable (Protestants and Evangelicals) were likely to experience divorce more than the general public. Barna states, "Evangelicals represent 12% of the adult population but 16% of the divorced population."
5. Dr. Peter Marshall, late Chaplin of the United States Senate (1946-48) in his inaugural prayer before that august body.
6. Ed Wheat, M.D., Gaye Wheat, *Intended for Pleasure, 3rd Edition* (Grand Rapids: Fleming H. Revell, 2001), 19. "Because all phases of the biblical plan for marriage must be in operation before we can fully enjoy the sexual union

as God designed it, we need to have a clear understanding of His plan."

7. Eric J. Keroack, M.D., FACOG and Dr. John R. Diggs Jr., M.D., "Bonding Imperative," A Special Report from the Abstinence Medical Council. As quoted by Abstinence Clearinghouse, 30 April 2001.

8. Jason Evert, If You Really Loved Me (El Cajon: Catholic Answers Inc., 2003) 8.

9. Neural Oxytocinegric systems as Genomic Targets for Hormones and as Modulators of Hormone-Dependent Behaviors, Rockefeller University NY, 1999.

10. Dear Abby, "Regretful Teens Advice Against Having Sex Too Soon," Indianapolis Star, 8 March 2001, E P. 4.

CHAPTER 3

THE CHURCH:
A FORTRESS OF VIRTUE?

On any typical Sunday morning, we can look out across the gathered congregation of any of America's thousands of churches and see that the crowd is a mixture of young and old. On the surface, it is good to see young men and women clutching their Bibles and raising their voices in praise as the congregation participates in songs and worship. In some churches, there are praise and worship teams; in others there are majestic choirs, and no one would be surprised to see the angelic faces of youth represented there. What lurks behind these innocent faces who humble themselves before the Lord each Sunday? Are today's church-going youth any different than those young people who are not found in church? Regrettably, with very few exceptions, the answer is that there is no difference at all. Statistics have shown that there is almost as much premarital sex among young people who are churched as there is among young people who never or rarely attend religious services.[1] It is not just with the youth; married couples in America have succumbed to the same grim statistics of social decay and divorce, as a whole, as the rest of the secular country.

What is this problem with sex and why has the church seemingly turned a blind eye? Why have most of our pulpits remained mostly silent while millions are dying of AIDS? Why have Midwest cities in the heartland of America become as bad as or worse than the *ultra-sophisticated* and immoral megalopolises of New York, Los Angeles, San Francisco and New Orleans? In America, we have two areas considered to be the Bible Belt; they include a stretch from Atlanta to Tulsa and from Cincinnati to St. Louis. The upper Bible Belt region is the Midwest heartland, and the southern Bible Belt region is the dominion of the Southern Baptists. Perhaps the problem lies with modern technology. We no longer live in isolated areas of the country where trends from Los Angeles and *sophisticated* New York would take 10 years to become accepted in the Midwest and sleepy southern towns. With the Internet, we can virtually be sitting in Frog Pond, North Carolina (an actual town) and instantly access the latest news from the British Broadcasting Corporation's London office. We could be sitting in Los Angeles and conversing through Internet chat rooms with people in Israel, Paris, Germany and Canada all at the same time. Television, through a high technology network of satellites, can beam in Billy Graham, Franklin Graham or pornography at the flip of a switch. Government schools "preaching" the faith of evolution[2] decry that we are here by an accident, that there is no purpose for our lives and question who should set the morals and whose religion we should follow. Professors of Naturalism teach there could never be such a thing as miracles. Is it any wonder that the cry of the sixties, "God is dead" and "If it *feels* good, do it," have filtered down into today's troubled youth?

When I was a young girl going to a Christian elementary school, I attended a party at a friend's home (whose mother was a teacher at my school). Two of my fellow classmates (one was the teacher's son) were found in a bedroom engaging in sex. I remember that the son's father opened the door, saw what they were doing, and then shut the door so they could continue their immoral behavior in private. Is the church a Fortress of Virtue?

In a CNN program, "Talkback Live," Mike Long, an abstinence education provider of Project Reality is quoted as having said, "The average age for marriage is 27 for men and 25 for women."[3] While it is true in our modern society that people are waiting longer to get married, it is not true that virginity is still expected in the honeymoon bed or what was once referred to as the bridal chamber. It has not always been this way. For thousands of years, it has been understood that men and women "saved" themselves for marriage. Virginity was the one present under the tree that was not unwrapped until it was time. It was special; it was anxiously anticipated; it was desired, and in the bridal chamber, it was consummated. This was a special gift that each spouse gladly gave to the other as if to say, "There is no one in the world like you and because you are so special, I have saved myself for this moment with you."

Unhappily, we see children having sex at younger and younger ages. It is no longer unheard of for fourth and fifth graders to have participated in a sexual experience to some degree. When I attended the same Christian elementary school, one of my peers in the sixth grade was caught having sex with another student in the church office. A verbal reprimand was all that occurred as a result of their immoral behavior. This Christian school was part of a mainline denomination and promised parents the upbringing and nurturing of children in the Word of God. This was not some public school where the teachers were afraid to walk down the halls and where God was ignored in the classroom.

One of my cousins married an ordained minister in another mainline denomination and later became ordained herself. They used pornographic films to enrich their sex life and saw nothing wrong with it. Again I ask, is the church today a Fortress of Virtue?

When our children turn to their elders and leaders of the community to have guidance and encouragement on how they should handle morality and sexuality, they hear flawed advice like that given by Ester Drill, cofounder of GURL.com. On the same "Talkback Live" program that we mentioned earlier, Drill states, "What we always say to girls is if you're not sure whether you should have sex, you shouldn't have sex."[4] This is like saying to someone regarding their eating, "If you're not sure whether you should eat, you shouldn't eat." In other words, if you do not have an appetite, do not eat, but if you feel the urge and think you are ready to eat, go ahead. This may sound like reasonable advice on the surface, but I know people who always have a craving for food and eat so much that they are obese. If they adhere to Drill's advice they would simply say, "I know I'm hungry and ready to eat, so I will." Who can say that they are not sure if they are ready for sex when their body is physically showing signs that it is ready because their heart is pounding and their emotions are running high? Historically, the answer given to, "When should I have sex?" has been consistent from ancient civilizations to the present time. From the Christian faith and other faiths, the wisdom of the ages has always been, "Sex is to be withheld until the commitment of marriage." On the "Talkback Live" program, Mike Long states, "… sex is a wonderful thing within the context of a committed relationship, particularly in a marriage as the standard, but if it's with anybody, anywhere, anytime I feel like it or I think I am in love, it causes very serious consequences. That's the truth we have to teach our kids."[5] We have just opened door a slight crack to say that if someone is not married, then they should at least be "committed." Long's answer was nothing more than a *politically correct*, conciliatory gesture offered in order not to be offensive to those who are cohabitating, a word that is more acceptable in today's *enlightened*, tolerant and diverse society. In truth, cohabiting is a sin. Mr. Long is accurate in his assessment that "… sex is a wonderful thing …" in marriage as the standard, and he is wise to reject sex being handled in a cavalier manner. To give credibility to "… sex is a wonderful thing within the context of a committed relationship …" gives a dangerous approval to those who want to play house but not have a mortgage.

While this may seem to be a small thing, small things can matter a great deal. For example, if a ship were to set sail from New York Harbor to Liverpool, England and follow a compass setting that was off by just a miniscule few degrees, at the end of the voyage, the ship leaving the New York Harbor would miss Great Britain entirely and wind up on the shores of Spain.

I fear for the girls I have counseled and for the young men who have been with them. I am concerned that it is just this type of crack in the door that has become a chasm which many have fallen into and they are unable to and they are unable to crawl out. In today's overly tolerant society, we strive to be inoffensive which is not necessarily a bad thing. However, when we are afraid to put standards and time-tested moralities into effect because we might "offend" someone, we are doing our society a greater disservice than simply saying that something is wrong.

Returning to the concept of sex in a committed relationship outside of marriage, young people and even older people fall in love, or at least for the moment they think it is love. This is no different with the people I know who have struggled with smoking. Smoking, like sex, once it starts, becomes a habit that is difficult, if not almost impossible, to break. A jokester friend said to me, "I bet you don't think I can stop smoking do you? I can stop anytime; I've done it dozens of times!" Therein lays the problem of saying that it is preferable to have sex in the "context of a committed relationship." I have had friends, both male and female, who have been very committed to people, sometimes for as long as a whole year but inevitably, without the vows of marriage, their relationships never lasted; yet, they were committed to one person—dozens of times.

What is happening to marriage in today's society? We see many Christian marriages, perhaps as much as 33% ending in divorce, a statistic mirrored by our secular society.[6] Perhaps with a closer inspection, we may not be shocked to find that these Christian marriages are not between couples who are chaste at the time of their wedding vows. They too become subject to the same sad statistics brought on by premarital sex as the secular (non-Christian) world because they began their married life with sexual baggage. It has been shown that marriages of people who were virgins at the time of their wedding vows rarely end in divorce, while the statistics for people who lived together before marriage, and this includes even those who never had sex with anyone else except the one they cohabitated with before marriage, show that the chances of their marriages ending in divorce is 80%.[7] These are not simply statistics for Christian marriages versus secular marriages, but rather they are a far more ominous revelation that sex before marriage is disastrous to anyone's marriage and is destructive to the families they create.

P.B. Wilson, in her book entitled, *Knight in Shining Armor*, makes a good observation with a word of great advice to couples who are serious about marriage and the trap that so many of them fall into during the courtship period when she asks the provocative question followed by her wise advice, "So what about the roses, romantic dinners, and soft candlelight? That should happen very close to the marriage."[8] Wilson explains a practical reason why a couple should wait until almost the wedding day before allowing themselves to engage in romantic pursuits. "Most singles devote most of their time to romance before marriage and then fall into a humdrum existence afterward."[9]

Attraction is nice, but looks fade. You not only need to build relationships, but you must also know what you are getting into before you make the final emotional and physical commitment that you should be saving for your wedding day.

Wisdom dictates that we should not open the door even a crack by saying that the criteria for having sex is to *preferably* be married, or at *least* be in a committed relationship, because the two are not the same—like the smoker who has quit many times compared to the smoker who quit once and never started again.

In the Bible, we find a woman who is having sex with a married man and is unceremoniously dragged before Jesus. The officials asked Jesus if she should be condemned for her premarital sexual relations. It is interesting to note that in those days, if you were caught in premarital sex (male or female), the Law demanded the sexually immoral should be taken out of the city gates and stoned to death. Usually, the first stone would be thrown by the individual who had the highest position in the community, at least a holy man who would be a pillar in the community and lead a moral life. Perhaps this was done as some kind of an honor, but the end result to the person being stoned was death. So now we have this woman who was caught having sex (although it seems the man inadvertently got away), and Jesus was asked if they should put her to death for her sin as the Law required. Jesus replied, "Let he who is without sin cast the first stone" (John 8:7). He then stooped down and started writing with His finger on the ground. It is even more interesting that we do not know what Jesus wrote, but we do know that those who were ready to stone her, from the eldest to the youngest, faded away and the woman and Jesus were the only ones left. The important part of the story is that Jesus did not accuse her, but He did tell her to go and sin no more. Perhaps this was the first time she had ever done something like that, or perhaps like many of the girls I have counseled, she just thought it was okay that one time like the person who stopped smoking over and over again. Whatever her background was, we really do not know, but we can probably assume she just simply enjoyed sex. It almost cost her life.

We do not stone people for their sexual indiscretions today, but it can still cost them their lives. Once AIDS has infected a person's body, they may be able to prolong the effects of the disease for awhile, but ultimately it can and will end in death. Other sexually transmitted diseases (STDs) such as syphilis and gonorrhea, if not treated in time can also end in death, or at least damage a person's body and health in such a way that it will forever alter some of their physical functions and/or affect their brain.

The woman in the Bible was fortunate. She escaped "that time" with her life, and she was given the opportunity to start her life anew with the wise instruction of Jesus not to continue in that lifestyle. Virtue was offered to her once again. By abstaining from sex from this point forward, she could live the life of and become a virgin again. Biblically, is this possible? We know that if anyone is in Christ, he becomes a *new* creature: "Old things are passed away; behold, all things become new" (2 Corinthians 5:17).

There is a lot of talk about the schools teaching "sex education," but the schools have already expelled God from the campus and while censorship is a word that no one tolerates, the Bible has been censored. If we teach sexuality from a humanistic point of view, which proposes that humans are, in fact, animals and animals have sex without morals, then who is to say that we should not enjoy our own sexuality as we see fit? We try to repackage it by redefining words and going through the motions of expressing a kind of morality such as, "It is preferable to wait until marriage to have sex, but (wink, wink) if you cannot refrain from having sex, then at least protect yourself." This message is really saying, "No one expects you to really wait, so here is how to keep from getting pregnant."[10]

Mike Long of Project Reality states, "I do talk about contraceptives a lot. I talk about them a whole lot. The difference is I do not present them as the answer because they're not the answer." He goes on to say, "I talk about how they will reduce your risk (and you're smart enough to understand that), but you must also understand that the risks are still there, and only you can decide if it's worth reducing that risk for a life-scarring consequence or disease or being 100% in control of your life and your sexual life and never have to worry about those problems and have all these wonderful things to look forward to."[11]

The important reality is that a contraceptive cannot protect your counselees from losing their virginity and like crack cocaine, they can become addicted the very first time. Your counselees may not get pregnant and/or may not catch a social disease, but their future marriage can become infected and possibly become terminally ill, thus ending in divorce. All the condoms in the world cannot protect from that, just like a shot of penicillin will not restore a broken marriage. The ones who suffer the most are the children who are ripped from a family that was once intact.

Finally, it is important for counselees to realize that even though our hallowed institutions and organized churches have drifted away from the moral centers that they were envisioned to be, they must remember, especially where the church is concerned, that buildings and institutions do not make up the church, but it is made up of the people of God who are called according to His purpose (2 Timothy 1:9). It is important that your counselees be directed to a Bible-believing and teaching church that edifies them through the uncompromised Word of God. The church is the people of God, and it is up to each individual to seek out for himself and put into practice teachings found in Scripture, and if your counselees' churches do not align themselves with the Word of God, you need to help your counselees find one that does. As every Christian counselor knows, a Christian is not defined by having a membership at a local church, but rather it is a personal relationship with the One who created and designed us to live our lives to be a reflection of His love and grace.

NOTES:
1. Barna Research, http://www.barna.org/cgi-/PagePressRelease. asp?PressReleaseID=106&Reference=E&Key=cohabitatio n "Morality and the Church" (16 March 2003).

The purpose of the church is to change the world from dark-ness into light, not the other way around where the world causes the church to conform to it. Jesus tells us, "... In the world you shall have tribulation: but be of good cheer; I have overcome the world" (John 16:33b). Paul instructs us, "And be not conformed to this world: but be ye transformed by the renewing of your mind, that you may prove what is that good, and acceptable, and perfect, will of God" (Romans 12:2).

2. Norman L. Geisler, *Baker Encyclopedia of Christian Apologetics* (Grand Rapids: Baker Books, 1999), 225. Geisler points out that evolution began with a few ancient Greek scholars. Previous to Darwin, evolutionary theories were basically from the pantheistic world (religions that believed in many gods). They had no substantial scientific reliability. It was Charles Darwin who developed the concept called "Natural Selection" which, on the surface, placed evolution into naturalistic science. With this alleged scientific credibility, the theory of evolution moved from pagan thought to Western thought. Geisler goes on to explain that most of Darwin's theory has been rejected, except for the natural selection aspect which states that the strongest survive. As far as the fossil record is concerned, in a century and a half there has never been found any consistent major chain.

3. CNN's *Talkback Live*, "Mike Long," 3 January, 2001.

4. Ibid., "Ester Drill."

5. Ibid., "Mike Long."

6. Barna Research, http://www.barna.org/cgi-bin/PagePressRelease. asp?PressReleaseID=95&Reference=E&Key=34%. "Cohabitation is Increasingly Common/Marriage is Still the Norm" (16 March 2003). "Born-again Christians are just as likely to get divorced as are non born-again adults. Overall, 33% of all born-again individuals who have been married have gone through a divorce, which is statistically identical to the 34% incidence among non born-again adults."

7. Research Alert, *Future Vision* (Naperville, Ill: Sourcebooks Trade, 1991), 43. The chances of a marriage lasting among

couples who live together before marriage have an 80% greater chance of divorce than individuals in a traditional marriage.

8. P.B. Wilson, *Knight in Shining Armor* (Eugene: Harvest House Publishers, 1995), 101. Wilson cautions that couples should wait six months for a "cooling off" period before committing to their engagement. Getting to know if the person is sincere about his or her Christian walk before marriage is important because your counselees do not want to be unequally yoked for the rest of their life (2 Corinthians 6:14). Marriage is hard enough without being in moral conflict all the time. Wilson wisely writes, "Your goal is to interview — not have intercourse."

9. Ibid.

10. George Barna, *The Future of the American Family* (Chicago: Moody Press, 1993), 133. In a study by the University of Wisconsin, it was discovered that those couples who live together are more likely to (as opposed to those who have never been married and have never lived together) see nothing wrong with premarital sex and are more tolerant of extramarital sex.

11. CNN's *Talkback Live*, "Mike Long," 3 January, 2001.

CHAPTER 4

ABSTINENCE MAKES
THE HEART GROW FONDER

G od mightily blessed Abraham, the patriarch of what was
to become the Jewish nation. He lived in the land of the
Canaanites. When his wife Sarah was of great age, she bore him a
son, Isaac. Not wanting his son to be unequally yoked with women
from the pagan Canaanites, Abraham sent his trusted servant, Eliezer,
700 miles to the land where the tribe of Abraham's father lived in
Paddan-Aram. It was important for Abraham's son not to have relations with women; rather he should save himself for the woman his
father would choose for him to marry

We know from Scripture that Isaac was a virgin. In Genesis 22,
God called Abraham to sacrifice his only son. In brief, the story is
that Abraham willingly set off with Isaac to the place appointed by
God. When they arrived, Abraham made an altar and placed Isaac
on it. At the last minute, God stopped Abraham as his knife was in
midair and provided him with a ram for the sacrifice. We learn from
this that God provided a substitute sacrifice and when God makes
a commitment or asks us to do something, it must be completed.
In this case, God committed Abraham to sacrifice his virgin son to
which he agreed. Once this commitment was made, the sacrifice had
to be completed. We know that sin requires a blood sacrifice and in

our case, it was fulfilled through the death, burial and resurrection of Christ, who was also a virgin. The second thing we learn is that Isaac was a virgin. The sacrifice must be made of an unblemished creature, usually a perfect lamb with no spot or blemish. Isaac was a foreshadowing of the Messiah to come. In the case of the Messiah, He was not in need of a sacrifice because He was perfect, a virgin and had never sinned. Because He had never sinned, He was the only One who could be presented as a holy sacrifice before the Father and deliver us from the sin we have all inherited from Adam (1 Corinthians 15:22; 45). He fulfilled the Scripture foretold in Psalm 22 and was nailed to the Cross (Psalm 22:16). In God's eyes, virginity is not just the abstinence of sex. It is a commitment, an attitude toward a godly way of life and a lifestyle that is set apart (i.e., holy).

In the land of Canaan there were many beautiful girls, and some might have even been more beautiful than the wife Abraham had arranged for Isaac years later. In marriage, there are more important things than just the outward appearance. Having sex appeal is not necessarily a bad thing, but it fades with time. People are like flowers as we develop. When the flower reaches the stage of a bud, it has not opened and has not become a flower. However, the potential of its beauty is apparent. The next step is when the flower unfolds; it reveals itself and all of its beauty and splendor. How nice it would be if all of the beautiful flowers that we pick on a spring morning would stay that way forever. Unfortunately, with the passage of time, the aroma and the loveliness begin to fade, shrivel and wilt.

While walking through a field, who would desire to pick wilted and shriveled flowers? We are drawn to the natural appeal of the young and blossoming flower. The point we are making is that in the land of Canaan there were many beautiful girls. However, beauty is only an outward appearance and temporary at best. While it is true that most people probably would not pick the old shriveled flowers, preferring instead the beautiful flowers that are in full bloom, some beauty may still remain in a shriveled flower. Things are not always as they seem, and we must look beyond the obvious outward appearance.

Consider the girl who has been given a beautiful corsage for her prom. It is lovely to look at and is a treasure to the young girl's heart.

After the dance, it is not uncommon for a girl to take the flower and place it between two pieces of wax paper, then press it into a book. Years later, when the book is opened and the old shriveled flower is revealed, memories of that special event flow forth from the time when that shriveled flower was once vibrant and beautiful. Yet, to the reminiscing girl, that shriveled flower that no one would pick up if they found it in a field brings back a flood of cherished memories.

This is how it is with people. A young man would not seek out someone who is older and toward the end of her life for a mate, preferring instead someone who is closer to his own age. Nevertheless, with the passage of time, the young girl who endeared herself to him will also begin to shrivel like the once beautiful flower. As the young man ages too, he will lose the bloom of his youth. When this older couple looks at each other, it is not the wrinkled skin they see, but the memories and love of their youth that has sustained them through all of the years.

It is prudent to pause for a moment to understand that when a couple is brought together and has Christ at the center of their marriage, the story I have just told is not uncommon. However, if selfish pleasures are the center of the home instead of Christ, the results are rampant divorce, broken homes and the eternal search, not for love through Christ, but for youth and pleasure from others.

The Bible is very informative about families, relationships, sexual misconduct and their consequences. In Genesis, chapter 15, God promised Abraham that He would bless his descendants, and they would be as numerous as the stars in heaven. However, in chapter 16, Abraham's aging wife Sarah, who had been barren through all of her childbearing years, still believed that God wanted Abraham to have a son in spite of her now being barren. So Sarah thought perhaps, as was the custom of that day, that Abraham could have a son through her Egyptian slave Hagar. Knowing that it was the common practice throughout the region, instead of praying about it, Abraham's hormones apparently were all too willing to believe that trying to have a child with Sarah's slave was not a bad idea. Under the stimulation of hormones, Abraham probably thought, "Sure sounds like God to me!" Therefore, Sarah's slave was impregnated by Abraham and she gave birth to Ishmael. Of course, this union was not blessed of God, nor was it God's plan for Abraham and Sarah. In spite of all of the negatives surrounding the birth of Ishmael, God blessed Ishmael, and the result is that the Arab people are his descendants. Remember, God promised Abraham that his descendants would be like the stars and the sand and whether right or wrong, Ishmael is also a descendant of Abraham. It was not until chapter 21 that the Lord visited Sarah and, "... Sarah conceived, and bare Abraham a son in his old age, at the set time of which God had spoken to him. And Abraham called the name of his son that was born unto him, whom Sarah bare to him, Isaac" (Genesis 21:2-3).

Perhaps it was because Abraham doubted God's Word to him that he and Sarah would one day have a child, so he impregnated another woman in an attempt to "help" God fulfill His promise that God saw fit to test Abraham. In Genesis, chapter 22, we read that God came to Abraham and told him to take his son Isaac and offer him on an altar as a burnt sacrifice. As we mentioned earlier, because Abraham was faithful and willing to sacrifice his and Sarah's only son and heir, God provided a substitute ram to be sacrificed in Isaac's place. God then promised Abraham, "... I will bless Thee, and in multiplying I will multiply Thy seed as the stars of the heaven, and as the sand which is upon the sea shore ..." (Genesis 22:17).

God was impressed that Abraham, now past a century old, was willing to offer his only son to God. However, Jehovah God is not a bloodthirsty pagan deity. Rather, He is a God of love and mercy who is sovereign and just. God made that wonderful promise to Abraham regarding his descendants because Abraham was willing to give to God, through his son, all that he ever hoped to possess or pass on to the world.

Abraham, being fully aware of the wonderful promise God made to him that he would be the father of God's chosen people, knew that nations were made up of people and people come from parents. Abraham, therefore, wanted his grandchildren to be from backgrounds who would honor God and not mix with people of corrupted faith or pagan beliefs. In those days, as people would marry and have children, and their children would have children, and their children would have children, that group of people (families) would be known as a tribe. Nations and colonies are made up of tribes. Several tribes form a nation. As we stated earlier, it was with that in mind that Abraham sent his very trusted servant, Eliezer, to travel those 700 miles to the land of his father's house. Abraham knew that it was important that his son's future wife be from the same tribe from which he came. He also knew that she must be a virgin girl (Genesis 24:16) who would marry his son so there could be no question that she might be pregnant by somebody else before she consummated her love and commitment to Isaac. However, as we previously stated, it was just as important that Isaac be a virgin too because God will acknowledge the descendants of a man whether or not in the eyes of the world they are legally conceived.

Thousands of years after the Bible was written, we see these God-given traits and gifts being passed down through DNA. The joining of a sperm and an egg is not affected by a piece of paper or even a religious commitment. It is a biological process. Therefore, God made it clear throughout the Bible that we are to keep ourselves chaste until marriage. We only have to look again at Abraham to see what happens when a union outside of God's will occurs, even though God may still honor the descendants.

We will now return to the nuptials of Isaac and Rebekah. When Abraham's servant reached the land of Abraham's father, the servant asked God to show him the future wife for Abraham's son. We will not go into how Rebekah became the bride of Isaac. We suggest you have your counselees read the story in Genesis, chapter 24. Abraham's servant knew that Rebekah was the right one for Isaac because of her virtue and chastity. Rebekah was willing to accept Isaac and travel hundreds of miles to a land she never knew for a husband she had never met. She had kept herself chaste, as had Isaac, and the marriage began. This was the second generation of what was to become the nation of Israel.

Through the story of Abraham, Isaac and Ishmael, we see that right and wrong choices in sexual relations can have long-term effects not only for the positive, but like ripples in a pond, the negative continues on long after the rock has sunk. Because Abraham and Sarah were not obedient to God's plan for the conception of their son Isaac, Abraham's descendants, thousands of years later and to this very day are still fighting over the land God promised Abraham.

When we wait upon God and honor Him by respecting our own bodies and when we prayerfully consider our potential mates, we have the promise of God's blessings for our descendants and ourselves (Genesis 1:28). If, on the other hand, we decide to take matters into our own hands and experiment before marriage, lives can unalterably be changed. We are not saying that God cannot make something good out of something evil as in the case of Joseph being sold into slavery (Genesis 50:20), but the quality and heartache would be far less if we had not ventured outside of God's will for our lives.

Having been raised in Los Angeles by a family who was heavily involved in the entertainment industry, it was not uncommon for us to have friends from this community. Sadly, the entertainment industry does not have the best reputation for high moral standards. However, God has and will continue to work mightily in Hollywood because of several well-established biblically-based ministries there.

A case in point for restored virtue: We have a friend who was the drummer for Stevie Wonder at a very young age and also was on tour for one year as the drummer for the Rolling Stones. As he matured both musically and as a man, he got his own recording deal and had a hit record. Expanding his horizons even further, he became a top record producer while dedicating his life to God. However, before he knew the Lord, he was having premarital sex with a young lady he was dating. (Many people equate sex with love, and they think that they have to have sex to prove their love.) Shortly after their relationship began, he dedicated his life to God and was convicted in his heart that sex outside of marriage was wrong so they began a life of chastity, much to the dismay of his girlfriend. She began to wonder if there was something wrong with her or if he was having affairs with other girls because he seemed to have lost carnal interest in her. Our friend explained to her that it was because he loved her and God that he wanted to wait until they were married to continue in the sexual relationship.

While this is very sweet and the biblical thing to do in light of Scripture, we can also understand her sinful human nature. Imagine having your favorite dessert, and someone all of a sudden takes it away from you and says you cannot have it anymore. Even though the reason is a good one for not eating that dessert, you cannot help but remember how good it tasted and sometimes when you are very hungry and the thought of that dessert comes into your mind, it becomes very difficult to deny yourself. Of course, if you had not tasted that desert to begin with, there would be no temptation, or at least not as great a temptation to avoid it. I am happy to report to you that our friends did get married, and now they have three beautiful children and a rare, stable Hollywood marriage because they honor Christ in their romance.

In the Bible, we read about a Hebrew woman who had two sons. They moved to a land outside of Israel because of a famine. While they were in their new land, their sons met some very attractive local girls and married them. Sadly, the Hebrew woman's husband and sons died. All the daughters-in-law had left was their Hebrew mother-in-law who they loved very much. Naomi, the Hebrew mother-in-law, was a godly woman who was concerned for her daughters-in-law because they had no children, and there were no other Hebrew brothers to marry and give them children, as was the custom of that day.

Therefore, Naomi realized that she must return to her people in Israel. Her daughters-in-law, who were still very young and lovely, should remain with their people with the hope of attracting new husbands. However, one daughter-in-law, Ruth, loved her husband's mother so much that she was willing to forego being with her own people and their gods. She told her mother-in-law, "I will go with you, and your people shall be my people and your God shall be my God." So Naomi returned to her people with her daughter-in-law, Ruth.

Ruth, who was no longer a virgin because she had been married to Naomi's son, chose to live a life of purity and restored virginity through a commitment to the One true God her mother-in-law served. In the land and among the people of her deceased husband, Ruth lived a life that was above reproach among his and Naomi's people and kinsmen. Because Naomi and Ruth were poor, to help bring in food to eat, Ruth would go out into the fields after they had been harvested by the workers and gather what little bit of grain had been passed over. Since Ruth was still very young, pretty and lived a life above reproach, a rich man named Boaz noticed her. Of course, Ruth noticed him too, but she was a godly young woman and did not brazenly flaunt herself at him. Boaz also led a chaste life. It was not his custom to chase girls or engage in premarital pleasures. It was through the wise counsel of Naomi that Ruth was able to find out if Boaz was interested in her as a possible wife. Because Boaz was the owner of the fields where Ruth was scavenging (gleaning), he said to Ruth, "Do not go to glean in another field, nor go from here, but stay close by my young women" (Ruth 2:7-8). Scripture implies that Boaz would never be alone with a woman (including his servants) because he valued his reputation and his honor as much as he valued a young lady's reputation and her honor. Through this time, Boaz showed his affection toward Ruth in the presence of his servants and others. She reciprocated but always with people around. Ultimately, this virtuous couple was married, and God honored Ruth's commitment to a restored virginity by giving her a grandson named David who would become King of Israel and a great, great, great ... grandson who would be the Savior of the world, *Yeshua ha Mashiach*. We know Him as Jesus the Christ.[1] As this story illustrates, God not only blessed the individual couple, but has continued to bless their descendants as a result of their faith-inspired obedience to Him.

Sometimes people who are living together outside of marriage are involved in church. They believe they are saved, but they also believe it is okay to live together outside of marriage. Because they are involved in church and Bible studies, they believe God understands and, therefore, forgives their lifestyles. We see this in our next example about another one of our friends who was a beautiful young recording artist who had a hit song that went triple platinum not just in America but in Europe as well!

She and her boyfriend were living together and attended the same Bible study we did. They regularly visited a very good church in the San Fernando Valley (a section of Los Angeles), yet they were still engaging in a sinful relationship. Fortunately for them, and older married couple who were their friends at church did not turn their backs or speak judgmental words that would turn them off to God. Instead, they took them under their wings and lovingly but firmly over time, convinced them that what they were doing was out of God's will. Our friend wanted to marry this guy so badly that she was willing to live with him. On the other hand, he loved her, but was a little bit timid about making a final commitment. We cannot speak for him, but we can understand why having everything that marriage has to offer without the commitment would certainly give him pause not to rush into marriage.

Finally, this couple offered to let our friend stay with them while her boyfriend continued to stay in his home. They continued dating, but refrained from having premarital relations. They realized that they had to confess before God that their relationship was sinful, and the guilt they had was from disobeying the commandment which prohibits fornication. In doing so, they committed to a chaste life of restored virginity before God until they were married. It is important to realize that the road to hell is paved with good intentions, but only through divine intervention and a commitment to serving God are we able to attain successful results. Of course, the desire for sexual intimacy in their relationship was still alive in their hearts, but they were willing to forego sex because they wanted to be in God's will.

What does the Bible teach about virginity and sexual intercourse? It teaches that it is very important for us to understand covenants. In Genesis, chapter 3, we are taught how we came to be in the fallen state in which we find ourselves. God showed His generosity to our ancient grandparents, Adam and Eve. He virtually gave them the entire world and control of everything on the land, in the sea and in the air. God allowed them to eat from any tree or any plant they desired, except for one, the Tree of Life (Genesis 2:16-17). People and animals did not kill each other since the whole creation was designed to be vegetarian. The killing and the shedding of blood was unheard of (Genesis 1:29-30).

Unlike some people would have us believe, sex is not a forbidden fruit. God skillfully crafted and designed sex to be something of pleasure, intimacy, love and the means by which a man and a woman are to be blessed with a family within the context of marriage.

Returning to Genesis, chapter 3, after Adam and Eve had eaten the forbidden fruit from the *tree of knowledge of good and evil,* they realized that they were naked. They would no longer be blessed by being in a naïve state of innocence. In verse seven, Adam and Eve "… knew that they were naked; and they sewed fig leaves together, and made themselves aprons." Making clothes out of a plant is not unusual. Many of us enjoy wearing blue jeans and linen shirts that are produced from cotton, which is a plant, and cotton holds up very well for a long time. If we alternate our wardrobe, we can have blouses and shirts for years. Therefore, plants are not a bad source from which to make clothes.

However, when God confronted Adam and Eve when He saw them hiding behind clothing made from fig leaves, He did a strange thing: "… the Lord God made coats of skins, and clothed them" (Genesis 3:21). Was God simply making a fashion statement here? No, the symbolism goes much deeper. When Adam and Eve made clothes out of fig leaves, they just used the common plants that were available to them, but when God covered their sinful nakedness, He shed the innocent blood of an animal, then took the animal's skin and covered their nakedness. Consequently, for the first time blood was shed to cover sin.

The purpose of this story in Genesis is to explain that from the very beginning of creation, covenants between God and man required the shedding of blood after sin was introduced into the world. However, not all blood covenants covered sin. Eight days after a male was born, he would be circumcised. This was not God simply allowing plastic surgery to cosmetically improve the appearance of an appendage of the male body because He designed it incorrectly; this has a deeper meaning. When the circumcision takes place and the baby is dedicated to God, the blood of an innocent has been shed as an outward sign of commitment to Him. Whenever an important covenant was made, innocent blood was shed. This was known as a blood covenant. Although the shedding of animals' blood was instituted to cover sin, even that blood was not sufficient for a permanent washing away of sin. That was done through God's own Lamb, Jesus, whose blood was shed on the Cross as the ultimate sacrificial payment for our sins and the *new covenant* (Jeremiah

31:31). However, that was not the first time Jesus shed His covenant blood. When Jesus was eight days old, He too was circumcised; thus His blood was shed under the *old covenant.*

Many of your counselees may have read and understand the story of the Passover when the Egyptians had enslaved the Hebrews, but God had other plans and was about to deliver them from Egypt. Moses prepared the Hebrews to leave, but the Egyptians did not want the Hebrews to go because they needed them for cheap slave labor. God was preparing for a terrible thing to happen to the Egyptian people so that they would allow His chosen people to leave. God told Moses and Moses told Pharaoh that on this particular night, the firstborn of the Egyptians and the firstborn of their flocks would die because Pharaoh would not let God's people leave Egypt. In order to protect the Hebrews from the death angel, an innocent lamb's blood was shed and its blood was painted over the lentils and the doorposts of the Hebrew huts. When the angel of death passed over, God spared all who were behind those doors.

The shedding of blood has always been connected with covenants. When a young female virgin first has intercourse, her hymen is broken and blood is shed. This shedding of blood produces the blood covenant sign of marriage between the young virgin and the man. This is no accident, but a deliberate design of God to consummate the uniting of the male and the female as one flesh. Whether or not one takes it lightly or is ignorant of what the consummation shedding of blood means between a woman and a man, does not change the fact that a covenant has been established. Sleeping with other men makes the woman a fornicator, which is a sin in the Bible, making her a part of an adulterous relationship with anyone (Exodus 20:14). An argument can be made that because she did not know the Scriptures or because she did not understand the meaning of what she had been doing, she would not be held accountable. Ignorance of the Law is not an excuse.

In her secular book, *Going All The Way*, Sharon Thompson relates that intercourse no longer carries a "… lifetime guarantee since the turn of the (twentieth) century when it was a token of betrothal in some communities" (clarification ours).[2]

Even in past centuries, the problem was that if a young girl lived in a large city, her fiancé could hit the road and disappear, thus breaking custom and escape his responsibility. Back in the middle ages, after the couple was wed, the bride and bridegroom would retire to the bridal chamber while the guests were treated to a large banquet. It was the duty of the best man to stand by the bridal chamber door and upon consummation of the marriage, the sheet with the blood stains on it would be handed to him. He would then hold it up as a display to all of the gathered guests who would cheer. The merriment and feast would continue.

This was not done to embarrass the young bride or to be crude. The custom showed that she was a virgin, and that they had consummated their marriage. It was with the consummation of the marriage that the betrothal was acknowledged as complete. For a girl to be a virgin was understood in those days; for her to be otherwise would have brought shame to her and her family. This also shows the value of the marriage relationship.

Is this just a European tradition or does it have biblical roots? The oral tradition of Judaism dealing with a deeper understanding of religious subjects was compiled in a book entitled, *The Mishnah*. In the chapter regarding the "Biblical Source for Kiddushin," Kiddushin 1:1 states, "A woman is acquired by three means ... she's acquired by money, contract, or intercourse." At first blush, it may seem awfully degrading for a woman to be purchased by money. However, this is not the same as buying a cow or a house. For example, the Christian church is known as the Bride of Christ, and the reason the church is the Bride of Christ is because Jesus paid a high price for her. The price He paid was His life. The coin He used to purchase us with was His blood upon Calvary's Cross.

In a footnote of *The Mishnah*, it states, "The Rabbis had to accept intercourse as a means of marriage because the Torah's text made it unavoidable, but they did not approve. In their view, sexual consummation of the marriage ... should follow public sanctification of the union." Another Jewish Sage, Bertinora, in commenting on this particular passage of the woman being purchased, states, "The text does not read, 'A man acquires a woman,' but deliberately says, 'A woman is acquired,' to teach us that a woman can be married only with her knowledge and consent. This is a fundamental principle of Jewish marriage."[3]

Not only was sex considered a form of betrothal in Europe and the United States, but when people decided to live together,[4] they were considered married after a short period of time had passed and the marriage was considered legally binding. When they found brides on the prairies, many frontiersmen did not have the benefit of a church or clergy to marry them. When they committed to live together, or cohabitate, their union was made legally binding as a marriage by what is known as "common law." They were considered married by the community, sparsely populated as it was. Therefore, we have the same chain of events taking place—a man and a woman who consummate their relationship through intercourse and by living together without the benefit of clergy or a rabbi, were considered married. As recently as the 1970s in the United States, common law marriages were acknowledged by half the states in America.[5]

With the dawn of the twentieth century, morals began to decline and common law marriages in America began phasing out. Shacking up was no longer viewed as immoral as more and more couples began living together for various reasons without the benefit of religious sanctions. It was with the moral bankruptcy of the 1960s that the sexual revolution began, resulting in the following generations to become like a cork on the water being tossed about with no clear direction. Think about this: If someone is ignorant of a nation called Japan, that does not mean Japan does not exist. Similarly, forgotten moral guidance that has served all of mankind since the creation until recent memory does not mean that the moral traditions and the Judeo-Christian teachings should suddenly stop having any relevance. Up until the twentieth century, divorce was rare, families were intact, murders in schools and suicides by the young were rare or nonexistent. Could it be the amoral attitude of the middle twentieth century that was supposed to free mankind has, in reality, condemned mankind? Abortions abound, children out of wedlock are now commonplace, and a virgin is as rare as a lifetime commitment in marriage. Divorce is the alternative in a marriage when sex gets boring. As counselors, we should recognize that with the onset of the 1960s women's movement, women have given up their natural estate of being a wife settling for the more demeaning position of being a concubine. As a whole, only the men have profited through this decline in morality. We did not discuss this topic in our companion book, *You Can Be a Virgin Again,* because of the general ignorance and ramification of what it means to be a concubine. For the benefit of counselors, we will discuss this in more detail in chapter 11 and leave it up to you to decide whether or not to introduce it in your counseling sessions.

Sadly, young people have been taught through television, motion pictures, music and advertising that sex is nothing more than a pleasant pastime and something to be enjoyed whenever the opportunity presents itself. This has destroyed the future of so many women. In reality, ownership of one's body is a pagan idea. Counselees need to know that they belong to God, and through Jesus Christ's suffering on the Cross, a great price has been paid for their souls. Therefore, it is imperative that they be good stewards over the physical entity God has temporarily given to them in which to house their souls. "He that gets wisdom loves his own soul: he that keeps understanding shall find good" (Proverbs 19:8). If they truly care about their eternal souls, they will protect their bodies from harm and sinful lusts because "the wages of sin is death" (Romans 6:23a).

The Bible teaches that we are new creatures in Christ (2 Corinthians 5:17). In the Gospel of John, Jesus explains to Nicodemus that in order for a change to take place in his life and in order for him to be acceptable and pleasing to God and go to heaven, he has to be born-again (John 3:3); but what does being born-again mean? For some of us, we need to have a new chance at life. There are women and young girls who truly desire to start over. If they could only have the chance to be virgins again, they know they would make smarter decisions the next time. They would be on guard against allowing themselves to be in compromising situations that would allow them to give into those smooth-talking guys for a moment of romantic *feelings*. When a girl looks back at her life of sex and mistakes, she cannot help but feel that she has corrupted the potential of the young virgin she once was. Obviously, it is not too late for a girl when there are no children because there is less pressure from guys. However, if she has children, the guys will probably think she is interested in sexual dating since she is no longer a virgin. This seems obvious to the guys because she has children, but it may not be as obvious to the female.

This is not as bad as it may seem at first. Your counselees can think of it as a process of "weeding out the bad stuff." If the supply of men the unwed mother is relegated to draw from consists only of those men who seek out women like her who have had children (because they falsely believe an unwed mother is an easy mark), then it would be wise for her to weed out those losers from the start. A word of caution for your counselees: When a woman constantly speaks of her commitment to Christ, she leaves no doubt about her Christian values. Some unscrupulous individuals may "humor" her in order to get close to her, and then begin dating, followed by breaking down her Christian commitment by seducing her. Your counselees must be suspicious of "Christian talk" followed by actions that give away the true nature of the individual they consider dating (or has dated a few times but is becoming doubtful of). Your counselees can judge the true level of commitment of those they date by how they pursue them for their sexual favors.

For your counselee who is single and has children, the reality is that having children makes it harder to convince the pool of eligible men that she has indeed restored her virginity and is committed to chastity. For her children's welfare, it is important that she cleanse her conscience and change her lifestyle because of her influence upon her children's lives. Children must be cherished, protected and loved, not be brought up under the influence of a sexually-promiscuous mother whose actions teach her children to continue in a lifestyle of mistakes like hers. It is not uncommon in some neighborhoods to find three and four generations of families who do not have fathers, grandfathers or great-grandfathers, but instead consists only of a line of women who have fallen under the same mistakes and the same trap of being unchaste.

We do not live in a perfect world, but that should not become an obstacle if your counselees truly want to become a new creature—a new person and a new virgin. This can be accomplished by being born-again through Jesus Christ. Peter explains what born-again means: "Being born-again, not of corruptible seed, but of incorruptible, by the Word of God, which lives and abides forever" (1 Peter 1:23).

When your counselees are young and attractive, life seems to hold such promise. Consider the word "attractive." The root of the word is "attract," which means "to draw" and when your counselees have their youthful loveliness they draw men to them. It is how they deal with this attraction where so many of them get into trouble.

In the very next verse Peter said, "For all flesh is as grass, and all the glory of man is the flower of grass." As we mature from child-hood to youth, we are like the grass and when we come into puberty, we become that beautiful bud—that promising flower. Even though old age seems like it may be a long time away, the time of our youth and attractiveness does not last. Peter continues, "The grass withers, and the flower thereof fades away" (1 Peter 1:24).

In the natural, men are predators and women are accommoda-tors. For men, it is the thrill of the chase, not the actual catching of the prey, which is the natural conclusion of the hunt. Women are nurturers by nature and have a longer agenda in mind than just a momentary tryst. They are the ones who are committed to caring for the very young and offering guidance during the formative years of their children. On the other hand, while not alone in the parental role, men are looked upon more as the providers and protectors from outside sources.

Men must address their sinful nature, which is to conquer and move on to a new pursuit. This is a carnal and sinful desire that must be addressed head-on. There is nothing unmasculine about a man wishing to contain his lust. To control one's emotions is known as self-control, which is a true indication of maturity. However, when one has only the boundaries of his own morality outside of God, it becomes impossible to commit to celibacy. It then becomes neces-sary for men to seek the divine intervention of Christ's power to be manifested in their lives in order that they cannot only gain control over their fleshly desires, but that they can also produce a righteous nature as opposed to a sinful nature. As Jesus cautions, God under-stands our weakness. "Watch and pray, that you enter not into temp-tation: the spirit is willing, but the flesh is weak" (Matthew 26:41). Yet, we are assured, "I can do all things through Christ which strengthens me" (Philippians 4:13).

Many mature and wise women have told me that they wish they had known then what they know now, meaning that if they could only have seen their mistakes and the results of the mistakes they made when dating as a young girl, they would have done things differently. Nevertheless, all too often in the heat of the moment our *feelings* take over, and we cannot think past the next kiss. It is important to remember that the children resulting from a sexual union are with you forever. Some may say, "Well, I can use birth control." This may be true, and this will prevent pregnancy to a lesser degree (people using birth control get pregnant every day, and it is just a matter of time before it happens again), but do not forget that birth control does not stop the first issuance of blood the first time intercourse takes place. I am not addressing the means of preventing conception. We are dealing with the hard biblical fact that when your counselee has sex for the first time with someone, she has entered into a blood covenant with that guy and with every guy thereafter. By having more than one sex partner, your counselee becomes nothing more and nothing less than an adulteress.

Whether or not your counselee has children, whether or not she has been married, or whether she finds herself single and desires to restore her virginity until God sends her the mate He has for her—the good news is that your counselee can restore her virginity.

It may sound like a fairy tale or just a dream that is too good to be true, but the fact is that if anyone is in Christ, he or she can become a new person. If this is something your counselee wants to do, he or she needs to realize that in God's eyes, when they accept Christ as their Lord, the old (your counselee's name) has passed away and (your counselee's name) has become the new person who is now living (2 Corinthians 5:17). If your counselee truly repents from their heart, God will honor them.

Among the hundreds of girls I have counseled, a few in particular stand out. One counselee I will refer to as Susan told me she saw nothing wrong with having sex with the guy she was dating. She said it solidified their relationship, and that there would be no loss or hurt if their relationship ended. Susan was eventually told by her boyfriend that he wanted to break up, and within a couple of weeks she discovered she was pregnant with his child. She put her needs first because she was man (self)-centered. She was committing idolatry because she put her own lustful desires before God or anything else. The sexual relationship that God designed to occur only between a husband and a wife was designed to create a bond and make the couple one.

Here is a person who has repeatedly indulged her body and her mind in a behavior unacceptable in the sight of God. When someone submerges themselves in these types of practices, they start out with warnings from their conscience, but as they proceed to ignore these warnings, their conscience bothers them less and less until they finally reach a point where their conscience has become so calloused that they are no longer troubled by it. Susan had surrounded herself with friends who also engaged in premarital sex which was another reason why she did not see her sexual relationships as wrong. Paul warns of this effect in Romans 1:28 where he states, "And even as they did not like to retain God in their knowledge, God gave them over to a reprobate mind, to do those things which are not convenient."[6]

Another counselee I will refer to as Lori, told me she had been "claiming restored virginity" for the past year. When I told her how great I thought her persistence was in abstaining from sex, she said, "Well, that's just until I meet another guy." Sadly, this cannot be considered restored virginity. It is simply an interlude between affairs. There is no commitment or acknowledgement of a sinful lifestyle. I was stunned and saddened because I wanted to encourage her toward a moral relationship. On the other hand, another part of me was not at all surprised since sex surrounds us everywhere we turn — television, movies, music, commercials, the Internet, etc. She struggles with the temptation of sex out of marriage because she thinks it is an "okay thing to do." She even admits that she does not get that much pleasure out of it, but it is a way to hold on to what she perceives as a solid relationship.[7] After all, the idols we look up to in the television and movie industries do it all of the time, so how could it be wrong? God makes it explicitly clear that we are committing a sinful act if we have sex out of marriage. When God brings down the New Jerusalem and allows those who are saved to enter and eat of the Tree of Life, only sinners will be left outside the gate and consequently, denied salvation. These include sorcerers (drug abusers), whoremongers (sexually impure), murderers, and idolaters (Revelation 22:14-15). We are also instructed in the Ten Commandments, "Thou shalt not commit adultery" (Exodus 20:14).

In Lori's case, would you say she is claiming restored virginity or abstaining from a sexual relationship? The answer is that Lori is simply abstaining from sex. There is a difference between the two. The difference is that by abstaining, she is choosing not to have sex for the present time. Claiming restored virginity is saying, "I do not want to have sex before I get married because I want to live a life pleasing to God, and I want to give myself completely to my spouse." Lori needs to realize that marriage, and the sexual pleasures it encompasses, were designed by God, and she should desire to be presented to her husband as Eve was presented to Adam. "And the rib, which the Lord God had taken from the man, made He a woman, and brought her unto the man" (Genesis 2:22). We see that Eve descended from Adam and never knew any other man. When she was presented to Adam by God, she was chaste in mind and she was pure in thought. Adam acknowledged the unity that was to be between this woman and himself as he stated, "... this is now bone of my bones, and flesh of my flesh ..." (Genesis 2:23a). "Therefore, shall a man leave his father and mother, and shall cleave unto his wife: and they shall be one flesh" (Genesis 2:24).[8]

It is important, when your counselees commit to a chaste life, that they do it for the right reasons. As we have seen in the previous Scripture, the architect of sex and marriage is God. The main motivation must be to please the One who created us and knew us from the beginning of time (Romans 8:29). Our commitment must be based on the desire to please the Lord who paid such a high price for our salvation. If we realize the seriousness of the sacrifice and love that Christ bore for our sake, it makes it more meaningful and understandable for us to desire to please Him first. By abstaining from sex with the purpose of restoring their virginity, your counselees become chaste. Chastity is a state of commitment of purpose and of restored virginity, not just a pause between sexual activities. I have known many people who claimed to have given up smoking between cigarettes and drinking between parties, but in reality they are still addicted.

God says in 2 Corinthians 11:2, "For I am jealous over you with godly jealousy: for I have espoused you to one husband (Jesus), that I may present you as a chaste virgin to Christ" (clarification ours). You need to enable your counselees to understand that God is saying if we are truly committed to Him, there is not an option of playing the fornicator because when your counselees are committed to someone, there is no room for sinful fornication. Temptation becomes a flickering thought that is rejected before it takes root. According to this passage, those who are married and have sexual intimacy within marriage can still be considered virgins because their sexual activity is within marriage and, therefore, may still be presented as the allegorical virgin bride of Christ. In marriage, we become one with our partner and, therefore, it is not considered fornication. Those who are not married and remain chaste will also be acceptable to the Bridegroom, Christ Jesus. As far as the world is concerned, when a man and a woman keep a covenant relationship of marriage, they are still virgins because the woman will not sleep with another man. From the viewpoint of some unscrupulous person who would try to seduce her, she may just as well still be a virgin because he is not going to get anything from her. The same applies to her husband. Your counselee may ask, "What if I am abstaining from sex with a *significant other* and the Lord returns? I have not had sex since I broke up with my last *significant other* so I should not have to worry, right?" Sadly, as biblical counselors know, your counselee will not be a virgin in God's eyes, in spite of her abstinence from sex because God looks at the heart, not how long it has been between affairs. Your counselee needs to know you cannot fool God!

Many of the young girls I have counseled are not Christians. Their rejection or ignorance of God's Word became very apparent because of the situations in which they find themselves. One girl I counseled came in with her boyfriend for a pregnancy test, and the test result was positive. After talking with them for awhile about where their relationship was headed, he said that he would be more than happy to pay for an abortion. It turned out that he had a seven-week-old baby by another girl and did not want anymore children.

What is wrong with this picture?! If they had simply not engaged in sexual relations, she would not have been pregnant. His actions would not have resulted with a baby by another girl. He said he did not want anymore children, but what about the expectant mother's say in this matter? Who will speak for the innocent child? God tells us, "Before I formed you in the belly I knew you, and before you came forth out of the womb I sanctified you ..." (Jeremiah 1:5a). What role does God play in this? Where were their values, and what motivated them to have sex with each other?

There are thousands of people in the world who have grown up with the belief that it was okay to have sex whenever they were ready for it; they were told to make sure that it was with someone they love and someone who would make it very memorable but above all, be safe. What is safe? Physically, a person may have the goal in mind to prevent catching a disease or hopefully avoid getting pregnant, of which there is no guarantee. People of all ages, young and old, are told to use condoms because they can protect them from pregnancy and/or sexually-transmitted diseases (STDs), but did you know there is a possibility you can catch sexually trans-mitted diseases from using a condom? A condom is simply tightly molded latex woven together to make a seemingly solid protective piece of rubber. Sexually-transmitted diseases and sperm can and *will* penetrate the latex material, so no one is safe unless they make a commitment to restored virginity. The reason the HIV/AIDS virus can penetrate the latex is that the HIV/AIDS virus cells are 1/25th the diameter of the sperm cell and *smaller* than the pores of the latex. Other sexually-transmitted diseases are also able to be passed on while using condoms, but it is not just condoms. In 1989, Dr. Sandra Samuels, Director of the Rutgers University Student Health Center, states the following, "Infection rates were equivalent regardless of the contraceptive method. Diaphragm and condom users had infec-tion rates of 44 percent and 35.7 percent respectively, whereas those using no contraceptive or oral contraceptive had infection rates of 44 percent and 37 percent respectively." That included other STDs as well as HIV/AIDS. Notice the chance of being infected is almost the same whether or not one had *protected sex!*[9]

However, the larger questions are, "What about the eternal consequences?" and "What about the devastation to your counselee's soul?"

NOTES:

1. It is important to remember the old adage, "beauty is only skin deep." Boaz was a wise and honest man. He realized the youthful beauty that Ruth was blessed with would not endure forever. What Ruth had that was far more attractive was her willingness to leave the land she grew up in and relocate in a place foreign to her (Israel). Ruth did this because of her loyalty and commitment to the mother of her deceased husband and the living God of Israel, a rare virtue indeed (Ruth 2:11-12).

2. Sharon Thompson, *Going All The Way*, (New York: Hill and Wang, 1995), 21.

3. Eugene J. Lipman, Translator, Title *The Mishnah* (Toronto: George J. McCleod Limited, 1970), 191-192.

4. James Sweet and Larry Bumpass, *"Young Adults' Views of Marriage, Cohabitation, and Family*," paper #33, National Survey of Families and Households, published by the Center for Demography and Ecology, University of Wisconsin-Madison. For every five couples who cohabitate in today's society, approximately three wind up in marriage.

5. Clarence L. Barnhart, Editor, *The American College Encyclopedic Dictionary* (Chicago: Spencer Press, Inc. 1959), 243. Common law marriage, a marriage without a marriage ceremony, civil or ecclesiastical, generally results from living together as man and wife: Henry V. Poor, Advisory Editor, *You and the Law* (Pleasantville: Reader's Digest 1977), 420-427.

6. Franklin Bookman Electronic *King James Bible*, Version 770. *Convenient*: proper, suitable or fitting.

7. Again, we see a person trapped in idolatry *and* the spirit of witchcraft, rebelling against godly morality to satisfy the desire for a mate through the lust of the flesh. "For rebellion *is as* the sin of witchcraft ..." (1 Samuel 15:23a).

8. It is important to notice here that Scripture says <u>wife</u> and <u>not</u> <u>wives</u>, and <u>one</u> flesh, <u>not</u> <u>two</u>. Throughout Scripture, we have seen multiple marriages, including Jacob and King David. However, these relationships were based on customs and not on God's design for marriage. Nowhere in Scripture does God approve of more than one wife, and your counselees must be careful who they marry because God does not approve of divorce (Matthew 19:9). Paul cautions Timothy that if he wishes to be a bishop, "A bishop must then be blameless, the husband of one wife …" (1 Timothy 3:2a).

9. Joe. S. McIlkhaney Jr., *Why Condoms Aren't Safe* (Colorado Springs: Focus on the Family, 1994), 2-7.

CHAPTER 5

CASE HISTORIES YOU
MAY BE ABLE TO RELATE TO

The following case histories, like all of the scenarios in this text, are based upon true events; only the names and events have been modified to protect the true counselee.

MELISSA

<u>Case History</u>

Melissa, an 18-year-old unmarried young woman, who considered herself a Christian but never went to church, complained, "I can't believe I'm pregnant! I just can't have a baby now. My fiancé, Mike, will kill me.[1] He's really looking forward to buying a new Porsche. He's always buying something for himself, but he never buys me anything! I don't understand how I could have become pregnant. I've been taking the pill. It's just not fair. I've have been fighting the genital diseases Mike gave me last month and now this! Mike has infected me twice in the past year. I'm so tired of him infecting me. It seems I'm always taking antibiotics. Why does he do this to me? I just have to get an abortion; that's all there is to it. Oh, I wonder what Mike will say. I need to ask him what I should do. I'm so confused. Yes, Mike will tell me what to do!"

Counseling Overview

Melissa's problems are several-fold. To begin with the obvious, she is engaging in premarital sex with a man who does not want to commit to her because he does not want to commit to God. Without God in any relationship, the focus on the partner is not as strong as the focus on their own desires and self. When we have a commitment to Christ, the biblical steps of a relationship and marriage are put into practice, which is a commitment to each other and refraining from sexual intimacy until God blesses the union in a public setting.

Mike does not want the commitment of marriage. In order for her move in with him, he is willing to appease her conscience by telling her that he will marry her if they live together first. Mike is even less agreeable to having children who, outside of the biblical view, become a burden to feed, clothe, educate, etc. This financial obligation takes away money that he might use on himself to purchase cars, clothes, jewelry, traveling and partying.

If this sounds selfish, it is. The only way for true happiness to be attained in relationships is to focus on what Christ desires—that which will bring Him glory and be pleasing to Him, not what we desire for ourselves.

As for Melissa, her focus is primarily on herself. She wants to attend nursing school, which is a good thing, and she should be encouraged to do so; but the reason she is going to school is for self-improvement (i.e., financial) so she can earn more money for a better lifestyle. She is taking birth control pills. This, too, is a focus on her. She wants to engage in sex without experiencing the natural result of intercourse, which is the responsibility of rearing children. She wants to have a man to share her life with and take care of her, but because he is not willing to marry her, she is willing to defend her own self-desire of having someone another way, no matter what she has to do. Therefore, the trade off of living with someone outside of marriage is a reasonable compromise for her to get her way.

It is obvious that Mike has had premarital sex not just with her, but as an ongoing lifestyle outside of the "living together" arrangement he has with Melissa. In this relationship, Mike is focused on his wants, just as Melissa is focused on her wants. Mike realizes that the living arrangement without commitment is just that—a living arrangement without any commitment. He *feels* free to satisfy his "needs" because there is no commitment to anyone. Since he thinks there is no God, he does not have to play by God's rules, and the only commitment he is really concerned with is him. Through his promiscuity, Mike, has infected Melissa with a sexually transmitted disease for the second time. This has complicated matters because the antibiotics nullified the effectiveness of the birth control pills she was taking.[2]

Melissa is at a crossroads about what to do with her current pregnancy. It is obvious she is not a virgin because she is now pregnant. One of the great myths of our modern society is that there are no absolutes, but people have an innate understanding of right and wrong even though they will not admit it (Judges 17:6; Proverbs 12:15). A classic example of this is when Melissa complains about her "fiancé." She believes that sleeping with her fiancé is okay, and justifies this by denying that they are "shacking up."[3] However, the sad truth is that Melissa is not wearing an engagement ring, and no date for a wedding has been set. This fantasy world she has built around herself is solely for her own desire of self-fulfillment. Pop-secular psychology refers to this sinful situation as having good self-esteem.[4]

As far as fairness goes, is it fair for someone who jumps out of an airplane without a parachute to complain, "I'm about to die and it's not fair"? Perhaps in the mind of the fool who jumped out of the airplane, it is not fair, but anyone who can connect the dots understands that jumping out of an airplane without a parachute is a foolhardy thing to do. Likewise, anyone who continually engages in intercourse (married or unmarried) will have to face the odds that she will sooner or later become pregnant. Perhaps the person jumping out of the airplane had done it many times before while flying 20 feet above the ocean; but in this particular instance, the plane was inadvertently carried to 1,000 feet above the water at the unfortunate time of jumping. This person may say, "It's not fair that a sudden updraft caused the plane to take a sharp climb just at the point when I jumped!" Maybe it is not fair, but jumping out of airplanes without parachutes is like regularly engaging in sex; sooner or later it will result in an unexpected ending.

Once the jump has been made, we can only deal with the immediate and the future. In Melissa's case, this does not have to be disastrous. She should not look to Mike for guidance, but instead seek God's guidance through His Scriptures. Melissa has made many positive and negative choices in her life. The fact that she wants to improve her lifestyle and become more financially stable by committing to studying nursing is a good choice. Seeking ways to improve our lives are not bad things to do. It is how you go about improving your life—by what and whom you seek—that determines your positive and negative choices.

Melissa's boyfriend is an atheist. Melissa must decide for herself what path she wants to travel. Jesus says, "I am the way, the truth and the life. No one comes to the Father but by Me" (John 14:6). In Deuteronomy, God admonishes the Jews by saying, "I call heaven and earth to record this day against you, that I set before you life and death, blessing and cursing: therefore choose life, that both you and your seed may live" (Deuteronomy 30:19).

Melissa has to realize that God loves her very much, and there is nothing that God cannot do in her life. We all sin and we all make mistakes, and most of the time the mistakes we make are actions of our own choosing for our own self-gratification. Self-gratification is not always wrong in and of itself. When we are hungry, we gratify our hunger by feeding ourselves. God does not condemn us when we satisfy our hunger by eating. As human beings, we all have sexual desires when we reach puberty and beyond; those desires are not necessarily evil. God wants those desires to be realized, but He gives us a framework that we call the nuclear family where we can express and gratify those desires and feelings. It is when we deviate from God's plan that chaos enters our lives.

Therefore, Melissa must decide if she wants to choose life by acknowledging Jesus as her Lord and Savior, who offers her the way, the truth and the life or reject the divine gift and seek after the world's ways. If she chooses the latter, only chaos will follow. In my counseling, it becomes very apparent that once girls commit themselves to an ungodly lifestyle, multiple pregnancies and reoccurring abortions become the norm for their lives.

However, if Melissa chooses Jesus (she is choosing life), she will be blessed and the life of her child will likewise be a blessing to her as God promised.

It is very difficult for a young girl who finds herself pregnant because many times the so-called "fiancé" she is living with breaks off the engagement and is never heard from again. Melissa must be shown that by accepting Christ into her life, even with the physical evidence of the loss of her virginity, which is manifested by the reality of her child, she can still restore her virginity and cleanse her conscience before God and be an example to her child and friends.

Ideally, as in the case of the entertainers we talked about earlier, through biblical counseling, Melissa and Mike could be led to the salvation of Jesus Christ and a commitment to premarital fidelity with the promise of setting a date for their wedding. This worked out great for our entertainment industry friends. However, the troubling difference between the two cases is that the drummer and his fiancée knew Christ, but had to acknowledge their commitment to serve Him first, which they did. In Mike's and Melissa's case, Mike is an atheist. If Mike decides that he wants to leave Melissa, she will not be alone because of her acceptance of Christ as her Savior; she will become His bride and He will give her the protection and guidance through His Word as though she were married to a godly man.

Unfortunately, reconciliation was not possible; Mike did leave Melissa. This was not a total surprise because the sad statistical fact is that once a cohabiting couple's sexual activities (or couples engaging in premarital sex) result in a pregnancy, the male usually deserts the unwed partner.[5]

At first, Melissa was furious—how dare he leave her in this predicament! After she calmed down, she finally admitted the truth that Mike did not want to be tied down with "some bratty kid." She reflected upon how she ended up in this predicament in the first place. She was using her body to entice Mike to love her and give her a sense of security. She really believed Mike cared for her in spite of the sex. She could not, or would not, bring herself to believe that sex was the main reason Mike hung around. While she wanted to be giving and withhold nothing from Mike in their relation-ship, Mike apparently thought otherwise. With a real commitment looming in Mike's life, he decided he wanted no part of it, much less any consideration of Melissa's needs.

After Melissa worked through all of the tangled emotions, I urged her to focus on what she knew as a more reliable place to begin sorting through all that had led her to this crisis, as opposed to relying upon her *feelings*. Melissa admitted that she needed to rely on something or someone more than herself. Through careful and compassionate counseling, Melissa began to see that she needed someone in her life who could save her from all of the grief she had brought upon herself through a life of sin. Once she admitted she was to blame because she willingly allowed Mike's entry into her body, she was able to release her dependency on the vain hope that somehow, someday, Mike would return to her. She needed now, more than ever, someone she could depend upon, no matter what she was about to endure. She finally realized that someone was Jesus.

Melissa now attends a Bible-teaching church,[6] as well as a Bible study and has restored her virginity. The church she attends has a support group which loves, encourages and cares for her, while at the same time holds her accountable. They have put her in touch with a ministry that offers her food, baby clothes and financial assistance. Melissa is also attending nursing school, and while she is still facing many challenges in her life because of her mistake, she is finding her life more meaningful and blessed.

CLAUDIA

Case History

Claudia is a 42-year-old divorcée. "I've been divorced for 10 years and have not dated very much because I have been concentrating on my career in the film industry. I have worked at (name withheld) Studios since I was in my early twenties and am now an assistant director. The problem I have is that on the few occasions I do go out, the men all want to have sex. They know I'm divorced and that seems to give them carte blanche to demand favors from me. I'm really getting frustrated because I want to go out and have a good time, but I feel pressured to have sex. I must admit that I do miss having relations since my divorce and have been tempted at times, but I'm frustrated because it seems that if I don't allow them to have some foreplay, they don't want to take me out again, and if I allow them to have foreplay, I'm afraid it is going to lead to a situation I may not be able to control. I'm not just worried about them, but I'm worried about myself too. I want to get married again, but most of the men I've dated have been married and divorced as well. I really don't know what to do. We live in a *modern* age where sexual behavior seems to be the norm and where everybody's is doing it, but I don't want to do anything that will displease God."

Counseling Overview

Generally speaking, the studio environment does not offer her a good source of eligible men. She must realize that she is a unique individual made in God's image and as such, has responsibilities of conduct that need to be pleasing and glorifying to God through her actions.

To keep from having temptations, she needs to find a ministry at her church, or one sponsored by a biblically-based church, perhaps a singles' group where she can interact and develop some good relationships (i.e., not just with the men, but with the single women as well).

She should date only Christian men and go to places that are public and moral. Double dates with other Christians are a good protection. When she goes out to dinner with her date, she should make sure it is a nice restaurant that is not connected with sleaze and avoid restaurants that are connected with a bar that features lude dancing, rock music, pool halls, etc. Environments are very important because they define the person you are by association. She must always think, "Does Jesus approve of where we are going and what we are doing?" This is necessary because Jesus *is also* on that date with her.

She complained that if she did not allow some foreplay, men would not take her out again. This is a counterfeit complaint. She should not want to go out with anyone who would even want to try to touch her body in an intimate place. Kissing can lead to heating up the hormones and should be avoided. If she finds someone she really likes and they have been dating regularly, a quick kiss on the cheek may be fine but not on the lips.[7] By setting high standards for her dates and herself, she will be making plans to maintain and protect her purity and not return to sinful situations for which she asked Jesus' forgiveness. Virginity is a gift from God; it sanctifies that we have been morally chaste and are clean and pure by not allowing the mind to think beyond what is acceptable conduct by God. For as the mind thinks, the body reacts, and if Claudia used to think that it was alright to be fondled a little bit, then she is defiling her conscience. Thoughts lead to actions, actions lead to *feelings*, and *feelings* lead to sexual sin. She must not allow herself to be alone with her date. Ultimately, she should not be on a date wit an unbeliever. "Abstain from all appearance of evil" (1 Thessalonians 5:22).

She must remember that a man will not respect her anymore than she respects God in her life. God loves her so much that He sent His Son who was willing to die on a Cross for her sins. She should not take God's grace for granted and continue in a lifestyle of sinning because that would be like crucifying Christ over again. Paul asks the rhetorical question, "What shall we say then? Shall we continue to sin, that grace may abound?" Paul's answer, "God forbid" (Romans 6:1-2a).

SALLY

Case History

Sally is 22 years old and a senior in college. Sally states, "My problem is that all of my girlfriends are sleeping around with all of the jocks on campus. Some are even having affairs with the teachers. When I first came to campus, I was 18 and just out of high school. My family lives in another state, so I didn't have them breathing down my neck like I did when I was still at home. I was invited to a few frat parties where there was drinking. I had never had sex or anything to drink before, but this was a whole new world to me. It was exciting, and it seemed like everything back home was so old-fashioned and everything on campus was so fast and *sophisticated*, which made me feel so grown up.

"At a party I met this really cute guy. Because I was drinking, I don't remember how it happened or when, but when I woke up about 4:00 A.M., I was in bed with him. I was really scared and shocked. I snuck out of the room and went back to my dorm. He called me the next weekend. I told him I was really upset at what happened because I was worried about what people would think but he was really cool. He said, 'We live in a *modern* age; we are not in the dark ages. A lot of characters on television do it, and everybody talks about it. We cannot pick up magazines without reading about it.' He told me to look at every single magazine that was at the checkout counter at the grocery store the next time I went shopping to verify that there is at least one article about sex on the front cover of almost every one. If I could find a magazine that did not have sex on the front cover, he would not pressure me to sleep with him again. Well, the next time I went shopping, I'd forgotten about what he said until I got to the checkout stand. Sure enough, almost every magazine I saw—whether it was for teens, health or fashion—had at least one article regarding sex and some had several articles. So I started giving serious thought to the idea that perhaps I'm growing up, and maybe sex is not such a bad thing after all. Many of my favorite TV and recording stars are having kids out of wedlock, and everyone thinks it's cool. So the next time he called me, I told him I'd like to go out with him, but I was still uncomfortable having sex and asked if he still wanted to see me. He said that was fine, he understood, and we started going out again; but after the third or fourth date I wound up in bed with him again. It then became clear that every time we went out we'd have sex. Actually, I didn't mind after I got used to it because it was enjoyable, and it was nice to have all of the attention.[8] I thought he really liked me and was committed to me until I discovered he had been sleeping with a girl in my biology class. I found out during a class break when a few girls were talking about some of the parties we'd been to, and this girl brought up my boyfriend's name and said how great he was in bed. I was crushed, and after that experience I didn't know what to do other than to dump the guy. Since then, I haven't really dated anybody—it's been three years. To be honest, I am getting ready to graduate and a lot of my girlfriends are either living with guys or are getting married. I feel so left out. I don't know what to do because it seems like all guys want just one thing."[9]

<u>Counseling Overview</u>

Sally is trying to fit in and experience what she perceives to be adulthood. She has allowed her safety factors to be neutralized by going to a college far away from home so she does not have to be accountable for what she does. If she had come to me for counseling when this first started, we would have worked toward her committing her life to Christ. I would have advised her that she is too young to handle the situations she is involved in, advised her to return home to live with her parents and commute to school. Unfortunately, most Americans believe in getting their children out of the house at 18 years of age. Other cultures have children, especially their daughters, at home until they get married and that could be at any age. Another alternative would be that she find a Bible-believing church near the college she is attending and get involved with a home fellowship where she would be accountable to the people in the Bible study. However, she is a senior and getting ready to graduate, so we must address the problems as they exist.

She must recognize that drinking alcohol allows something other than the Holy Spirit to take control of her body, and she is using alcohol as an excuse to relinquish the blame of her own actions by allowing herself to be victimized by her drinking. This is a cop-out because she has the choice of whether or not to have the first drink.

Sally's excuse is, "I was invited to a few frat parties where there was drinking. I had never had sex or anything to drink before, but this was a whole new world to me …. Everything on campus was so fast and *sophisticated*, which made me feel so grown up." Even though Sally is in college, she is not using her brain. She is relying upon her *feelings*. Being on a college campus fresh out of high school leads some to believe they have entered an intellectual and *sophisticated* world. We only have to look at the Bible to find another group of people who saw themselves as intelligent and *sophisticated*.

Sodom and Gomorrah were the *modern* and *sophisticated* cities of their time. In fact, these two cities strikingly parallel the society where we find ourselves today. Sex was a pastime and homosexuality and bisexuality were looked upon with great acceptance and even favor. Homosexuals are demanding and receiving preferential treatment. In the days of Sodom, and Gomorrah, some angels came to spend the night in the home of Lot: "But before they lay down, the men of the city, even the men of Sodom, compassed the house round, both old and young, all the people from every quarter: and they called unto Lot, and said unto him, where are the men which came into Thee this night? Bring them unto us, that we may know (have sex with) them" (Genesis 19:4-5, clarification ours). Lot even offered his virgin daughters to be used for their sexual pleasures if they would just leave the men alone under his roof which they refused to do (vv. 8-9). This is the same wickedness that our country glorifies in movies and television disguised as *sophisticated* tolerance; but this is the same kind of wickedness for which God destroyed Sodom and Gomorrah (vv. 24-25).

Sally believes her experiences are *sophisticated* and *modern*, but it is simply the repackaging of people's sinful nature. Solomon, the wisest man of all time states, "The thing that has been, it is that which shall be; and that which is done is that which shall be done: and there is no new thing under the sun" (Ecclesiastes 1:9).

By studying the past, we are able to see the future. By observing how people conducted their lives in good ways, noble ways, evil ways, and sinful ways, we can see what the results will be for us if we choose to live a certain lifestyle. The source for us to study that will show us how to conduct our lives in a positive manner, as well as teach us the consequences of poor lifestyle choices is profoundly made clear in the Scriptures, God's Holy Word. We have no excuse to claim "victim" status, as secular pop-psychology would have us do, because the Bible exposes man's nature and the penalties and rewards for such nature. There are those who say, "This is not fair because not everyone has a Bible to read and, therefore, become victims out of their ignorance." However, this is not a valid excuse because Paul teaches us, "For the invisible things of Him from the creation of the world are clearly seen, being understood by the things that are made, even His eternal power and Godhead; so that they are without excuse" (Romans 1:20). People around the world know certain behaviors are wrong because their God-given conscience tells them so.

Just by observing life, we are able to see that certain lifestyles lead to destruction. The campus party scene results in poor grades, unwanted pregnancies, a dependency on alcohol and falling in with the wrong crowd. This results in immorality, all in the name of *sophistication.*[10]

Sally recaps what occurred at one of the parties: "Because I was drinking I don't remember how it happened or when, but when I woke up about 4:00 A.M., I was in bed with him." She said that at first she was shocked, embarrassed and was worried about what people would say but he said, "… we live in a *modern* age, and that we are not in the dark ages. A lot of characters on television do it, and everybody talks about it. We cannot pick up magazines without reading about it."

Her boyfriend was attempting to justify their actions, but all he did was give evidence of a very perverted world. The television shows that feature sex also show violence, and the soap operas are a never-ending merry-go-round of "changing bed partners." There is no stability, and the plots are always in turmoil, which keeps the viewer guessing and tuning in each day to see how the different characters' lives are "progressing." The fallacy of judging morals by what television offers is morally bankrupt. The average person is rarely seen on these shows. These beautiful people never complain about genital herpes, syphilis or gonorrhea. They very seldom, if ever, touch upon the subject of AIDS unless it is in a sympathetic role to show the homosexual as a hapless victim. They never show a woman having to deal with abortion or the emotional breakdowns that eventually follow the hapless mother who suffers post-abortion syndrome.

Certainly, television, movies, and magazines put on the mask of glamour to cover the truth of the hideous face of despondency, ugliness, and hopelessness which are the faces of reality.

Isaac Newton taught us, "For every action, there is an equal and opposite reaction." This is not only true of physics, but of human actions as well. When we do and say good things, generally good things will follow. When we do and say evil things, why are we surprised when hurt and despondency are a result? "For they have sewn the wind and they shall reap the whirlwind" (Hosea 8:7a).

Sally was persuaded to look at every magazine, and if she could find a magazine that did not have sex mentioned on the front cover, she would not be pressured to sleep again with the guy she met at the party. He had convinced her that immorality was normal, and that she could base her lifestyle on the approval given to sex through the popular magazines at the checkout counters. This is all too common in our society, and many people are validating their immoral lifestyles by just such excuses, and society approves of it, so it must be okay.

Jesus says, "Heaven (the stars) and earth shall pass away, but My words shall not pass away" (Matthew 24:35, clarification ours). Long after the magazines and newspaper articles have found their way to the bottoms of birdcages and are relegated to the trash heap, the particular advice and insights they have given will long be forgotten. It is only the Bible that offers us God's beneficial, timeless and life enriching truths. "All Scripture is given by inspiration of God, and is profitable for doctrine, for reproof, for correction, for instruction in righteousness" (2 Timothy 3:16).

Once Sally understood this, she was able to begin working on scriptural homework to restore her life and her attitudes, and very importantly, she began to restore her virginity.

<u>SUSIE</u>

<u>Case History</u>

Eighteen-year-old Susie is not a Christian, has one child out of wedlock and works at a convenience store. "My problem is that I dropped out of high school in the eleventh grade. I became pregnant by a guy who told me how much he loved me. I told him that I didn't want to have sex, but he kept insisting that if I really loved him it would be alright. He always used protection, but sometimes it would slip off. One time it even ripped, but it seemed to be okay because I didn't get pregnant. We'd been having protected sex without any "accidents" for about a year when all of a sudden, I missed my period. I was really disturbed, but he assured me that he really loved me. Now it was time for him to prove his love for me. When I told him I was pregnant, he got really mad and hit me. He said it was my entire fault and stormed out of the house. I've not seen him since.[11]

"Since I work the third shift at a convenience store, I meet a lot of guys who are getting off of work around that time, and a couple of them have asked me out when I was at the end of my shift. I really feel so tied down because I have to pay a baby-sitter to watch my child while I work, and I'd like to get out and have a little fun once in awhile. Sometimes, I am able to have the baby-sitter stay a couple of extra hours so I can go out. I am 18 now, even though I look older, and I can get into bars. (Susie lives in California where guys ands girls 18 are allowed into bars with escorts over 21 if the 18 to 20-year-olds do not drink.) The problem is that after I go out a couple of times, the guys find out I have a kid and because I wasn't married when I gave birth, they think I'm an easy girl. It's really hard to find a guy who will take you out if you don't give him what he wants.[12] I want to marry a guy who has an education and isn't a high school dropout like me, and I really want a guy who doesn't want to have sex, but they all insist on it. I'm afraid of getting pregnant again, but I keep thinking that if I give them what they want, sooner or later one of these guys will really fall in love with me and we'll get married. So far, they only take me out a couple of times, get what they want and never call me again. I'm just so hurt that I don't know what to do. Sometimes, I wish I were dead. I even think about killing myself, but I realize that would leave my daughter without a mother or a father. I admit that's a pretty stupid and selfish way to think. What's going to happen when my daughter gets older and sees me with these guys? I don't want her to turn out to be like me, and I don't want her life to be ruined like mine. I'm just so desperate. I want to be loved, and I want someone to take care of me. Can you please help me?"

Counseling Overview

Susie's problem is that she is ruled by Susie. This is self-centered and may seem justified on the surface because she comes from a broken home, but while an unfortunate childhood can be a factor for failure, it is not a legitimate excuse. Because we often believe we are victims, we give ourselves permission to fail. The truth is that it is easy to fail. Reasons abound, but not to fail requires commitment and dependency on God. Many people use excuses that they think gives them permission to lead a life that repeats mistakes. Many times young people, especially women, feel they have been deprived of love. Some Freudian and neo-Freudian secular psychiatrists try to convince us that if a girl does not have the masculine approval of her father, she will use her body as a means of acquiring a man's affection as a pseudo (counterfeit) father figure. According to secular psychiatrists, this allows for her misconduct because she is a victim and is, therefore, being used by men due to her unjust upbringing. Once again, we are allowing for people to continue in ungodly lifestyles because it is not their fault; they are just victims and, of course, a victim is helpless by its very definition.

We have been told by secular psychology that we should delve into our past to help us cope with our problems. As long as we are focused on events that have occurred and cannot be changed, we are wasting our time. What matters are not our individual histories, but how we are dealing with our present because what occurs today becomes tomorrow's history. Therefore, what we do today *will affect* our future.[13] A problem that young girls face with young men is the ever-popular line, "If you really love me, you'll do it." Some of the girls never think to say to the young man, "If you love me, you'll not ask me to do it!"

Traditionally, in all societies of recorded history, the one thing that a young woman had to offer, regardless of her socioeconomic position, was the purity of her body to the man who would become her husband. It is no wonder that even in pagan and heathen societies a woman's virtue (virginity) was considered a sacred trust since it was proof that she could make a commitment to the one she loved, even before she knew of his existence, much less having met him. This is the type of commitment upon which intimate relationships and trust have historically been built.

Virginity is an equal opportunity at birth, and what we do with it will affect the rest of our lives, not only for the young woman, but equally so for the young man who will pledge his fidelity (virginity) to her. Virginity is a God-given condition that we have from birth, and it is our right to maintain it until a commitment of marriage. In the garden, it was Adam and Eve's right to a life of purity in a pure and perfect world. However, through rebellion, they chose to throw this right of a perfect world away. Virginity is a lasting symbol of that perfect and unblemished state until, like our first parents, we either choose to keep it or throw it away. In this regard, we may conclude that our virginity is a type of birthright to be cherished or rejected. If some depraved individual were to rape a baby, he would be taking away the virginity which that child has a right to have until she is old enough to decide for herself whether or not she wants to remain pure until she is married to engage in sex. Therefore, in this regard, virginity is a birthright of every sexually-immature child. When someone is sexually mature, she still has the right to remain a virgin until marriage. No one has the right to forcibly take virginity away from someone through rape. It is their right to physically remain a virgin until marriage, for those who do not want to maintain their virginity until marriage, they must be willing to pay the consequences. We have the right before marriage to expect the person to whom we are engaged to be a virgin from birth, and they have the right to expect the same from us. In this sense, virginity is a rightful condition we all have from the moment we are born. Any type of birthright is something that is so important that the casual tossing away of it comes with major costs.

Remember the story of the twin brothers, Jacob and Esau? Esau was governed by his *feelings* and was willing to jeopardize a lot for the sake of a moment of gratification. His shrewd brother, Jacob, manipulated his desire for gain. Once Esau had given into his fleshly desires, he could never go back and undo the forces he had put into motion. The ramifications of what he allowed himself to participate in had far-reaching consequences that are still occurring in the Middle East today.

In the footnotes of one Bible version, we read in Genesis about the two brothers. "The fate of Esau serves as a solemn warning to anyone who forfeits permanent spiritual blessings for immediate passing fleshly gratification. Once a choice is made and acted on, its consequences cannot be reversed, and the blessings that may have been realized are lost forever."[14]

Here are two brothers. The oldest brother was named Esau and the younger one was named Jacob. Traditionally, the oldest son inherits the fortune and blessing of his father. God made a covenant with Abraham and with his son, Isaac (Genesis 17:19; 21). The blessing of God (Genesis 12:3) was to be handed down to all of the descendants of Abraham. However, there were certain blessings that were reserved for the oldest child. In this case, it was the direct lineage of Abraham, Isaac and Jacob that would lead to the blessing of the long-awaited Messiah who would be a blessing to the whole world. According to the prophetic Scripture, the Messiah would have to be from a straight lineage, as specified in the Bible and would be a descendant in the line of succession, traditionally from eldest son to eldest son.

For the moment, Esau, Jacob's older brother, was more interested in succumbing to his lusts. He did not think of long-term repercussions. Esau was only interested in the moment of gratification. His brother, Jacob, knew Esau's shortcomings and was only too glad to manipulate him for his own gain. He knew that Esau would trust him because he was his brother and would be led by his desires, rather than by his intellect. One day Esau came in from the field and came upon his brother, Jacob, who was sitting by a freshly-made bowl of pottage (stew). Esau was very tired and hungry and thought only with his stomach. Jacob, who was much shrewder, was clever enough to manipulate Esau's desires to his own advantage.

The story is as follows: "And Esau said to Jacob, 'Feed me, I pray Thee, with that same red pottage; for I am faint:' … And Jacob said, 'Sell me this day Thy birthright.' And Esau said, 'Behold, I am at the point to die: and what profit shall this birthright do to me?' And Jacob said, 'Swear to me this day;' and he swear unto him: and he sold his birthright unto Jacob" (Genesis 25:29-33).

The fate of Esau serves as a solemn warning to anyone who forfeits permanent spiritual blessings for immediate gratification and temporary desires. Once such a choice is made and acted upon, its consequences cannot be reversed, and the blessings that may have been realized are lost forever.

When Susie said, "I keep thinking that if I give them what they want, sooner or later one of these guys will really fall in love with me and we'll get married," she was focusing on herself ("… if I …") and her willingness to compromise her body sexually in the flawed reasoning that her promiscuity would entice a man to marry her. Therefore, she will continue in a hopeless spiral of sexual degradation in the vain hope that she will win in the end.

Susie has a vast emptiness in her soul which she is trying to deal with in the wrong way. She is lonely and hurting. She needs to be loved and be able to love. Susie is too focused on herself. Consequently, she is not allowing herself to have the love only God can give her—His love! Susie has been trying to capture the type of father figure she longed for so much in her youth, but she is going about it incorrectly. She will never find the perfect father figure here on earth. She needs to seek her heavenly Father who is the perfect role model for all of the fathers here on earth. Unfortunately, some men do not know God or understand what it really means to be a godly father, and this causes many children to be fearful of God the Father. How can Susie find her heavenly Father? The Bible shows the love of God through His Son Jesus who tells us, "… he that has seen Me has seen the Father" (John 14:9b). To get to know God, Susie needs to be in a Bible-believing church and become involved with a fellowship of godly women. God never purposed that Susie should feel abandoned. He knew her before she was born. He watched her as she developed in her mother's womb, and there is no place she could ever go where God would abandon her.

Where shall I go from Your Spirit? or whither shall I flee from Your presence? If I ascend up into heaven, You are there: if I make my bed in hell, behold, You are there. If I take the wings of the morning, and dwell in the uttermost parts of the sea; Even there shall Your hand lead me, and Your right hand shall hold me. If I say, Surely the darkness shall cover me; even the night shall be light about me. Yea, the darkness hides not from Thee; but the night shines as the day: the darkness and the light are both alike to Thee. For You have possessed my reins: you have covered me in my mother's womb. I will praise Thee; for I am fearfully and wonderfully made: marvelous are Your works; and that my soul knows right well. My substance was not hid from Thee, when I was made in secret, and curiously wrought in the lowest parts of the earth. Your eyes did see my substance, yet being unperfect; and in Your book all my members were written, which in continuance were fashioned, when as yet there was none of them. How precious also are Your thoughts unto me … (Psalm 139:7-17a).

God loved us so much that He came to earth and clothed Himself with a body of flesh so we could relate to Him and understand that He was tempted in the same way we are. Because God loved Susie, He gave His only Son, Jesus, who would not only come to earth to relate to her as a human, but to also pay the price for her sins with His very life. Susie needs to realize that God made her a special person and has a purpose for her life. If she would only put God above her own desires and seek the He desires for her life, she would no longer be lonely and she would be able to overcome her problems.

JOE

Case History

Men have trouble too, of course. I was advised by a friend about a young man we will call Joe. A military guy, Joe came from a genuine Christian family, but once he was in the military he became influenced by some of his buddies. The first year that he was in the service they kidded him and called him the "deacon" because he was such a "prude" about sex. After awhile, his buddies fixed him up with a girl and before he realized it, he had succumbed to a routine of looking for and having sex. He had a chaplain friend he worked and spent a lot of time with, so pretty soon, through the influences of the chaplain, Joe realized that his behavior was not all that great, and he wished he had not started. One night, while he was in his quarters, a female recruit came to the door and immediately put the make on him. She began fooling around with him and led him into the bathroom where she undressed and turned on the shower. Joe said they had a night of sex and when he woke up in the morning, he was really disgusted with himself. Even though it was a night of pleasure that a lot of guys would have killed for, he said he felt really dirty and ashamed of what he had done. At that point, he made a commitment not to have anymore sex until he was married. He kept that promise and when he left the Army, he enrolled in a Christian college. He has maintained that commitment ever since and is looking forward to going back into the military service—a life he loves, but wants to attend seminary so that he can re-enlist as a chaplain. I have seen a photograph of him, and he is not a wimp. He has a great physique and a handsome face. Now he realizes the importance of saving himself for marriage and in spite of the fact that he is no longer a "virgin," he has decided that through God, he can be restored. He has made that commitment before God and all of his buddies. He is on his way to fulfilling his dream of being an Army chaplain, and there is no doubt in my mind that he will fulfill his second dream of remaining a restored virgin until his wedding night.

This is an interesting case because over 3,000 years ago the Bible gave us advice which deals with this type of problem and yet, it is as up-to-date now as it was back then. In Proverbs 7 we read, "And behold among the simple ones, I discerned among the youths, a young man void of understanding. Passing through the street near her corner; and went the way to her house, In the twilight, in the evening, in the black and dark of night ... there met (with) him a woman with the attire of a harlot, and subtle of heart" (Proverbs 7:7-10). Solomon is preparing to tell us the story of a naïve and *unsophisticated* young man who falls into temptation and sexual indiscretion. Although he is naïve, he is smart enough not to want to be seen by the good people of the town because he is feeling guilty and is thereby seeking out his sexual partner under the cover of darkness. "With her much fair speech she caused him to yield, with the flattering of her lips she forced him. He goes after her straightway as an ox goes to the slaughter, or as a fool to the correction of the stocks (a means of imprisonment); Till a dart strike through his liver; as a bird hasteth (moves quickly) to the snare, and knows not what it is for his life" (Proverbs 7:21-23, clarification ours). We see that through his addiction, probably through a fantasy life of masturbation, culminating with a real sexual encounter, the young man opens himself up to all sorts of dangers. He is unable to control himself anymore. His lusts and *feelings* drive him into her arms like a bird who is hungry and finds food on the ground, not realizing it is about to be trapped in a cleverly laid snare. Furthermore, he gives no thought to the dangers of his life resulting from any sexually transmitted diseases. He has succumbed to his driving lust for sex, so much so that he has become foolish and careless. He is no longer thinking, but instead he is reacting to his feelings. It is not important just to *feel* good. You cannot rely on *feelings* alone because most of the time *feelings* will betray you. Solomon concludes, "Harken unto me now therefore, O you children, and attend to the words of my mouth. Let not your heart decline to her ways, go not astray in her paths. For she has cast down many wounded: yes, many strong men have been slain by her" (v. 24). Solomon points out to the youth he is addressing to listen carefully to what he is saying and not be tempted by lust and give into sexual desires. He warns that what you think of as a moment of love and what you perceive to be a desirable sexual union is only a deception because when you sleep with someone, you can be sure your partner probably has many other lovers to which you have become exposed. He concludes that for the sexually immoral, the path only leads to an eternity of hell. "Her house is the way to hell, going down to the chambers of death" (v. 27).

After a night of promiscuity, the serviceman (Joe) was convicted in his heart by the Holy Spirit that what he did was displeasing to God and he repented (turned away and proceeded in a different direction). He was thereby putting off his desire for lust and putting on a new commitment with a Christ-pleasing lifestyle. Joe could have shrugged it off and continued in his immoral lifestyle, but deep down inside he had truly committed himself to Christ. That commitment, through the prompting of the Holy Spirit, rose up to the surface and enabled him to repent and start a new life. With God, there is always hope for a new beginning.

DAVID

Case History

In our society, there is not a place where sexual indiscretions are not manifested. A junior high youth pastor told me, "You would not recognize some of the kids who came to the Wednesday night meetings professing to be Christian kids. From the very beginning, it was apparent that some of the boys were there just to pick up chicks."

The youth pastor says, "David started dating several of the girls. Later, one of the girls he dated came to me with complaints about his dating activities so, as his youth pastor, I began observing him and his activities within the youth group. I was troubled when I found out that some of the girls in the group had sex with him."

This creates a real problem for youth pastors because it is important to not turn kids away, especially those who really need the help. At the same time, he has an obligation to protect his flock. He found out that this boy had come from a broken home. His father read a lot of "girlie" magazines that were in the house, and his father was abusive to him by saying that he was not a real man until he had a real woman.

The youth pastor continues, "I confronted this young man and after counseling with him for awhile, I found out that he really loves and respects his mother. I told him that every girl who has intercourse has the potential of becoming a mother. I asked him how he would feel if he got one of these girls pregnant and 20 years from now had a son or daughter who loved their mother just as much as he loved his. They might grow up without a father. (The boy was only 14 and could not get married or support a wife and child.) At first he laughed it off, thinking I was putting him down. Then, he began to realize that I really cared, not only about the girls who might get pregnant and for the possible illegitimate child, but I cared for him as well."

Counseling Overview

The fundamental purpose is to have a right relationship with God and realize that sin is a condition of the heart and an indication of our relationship with God. Using Scripture, the pastor showed David how God desired to choose a wife for a young man. He also shared the story in Genesis 24 of how Abraham realized that his son Isaac was becoming mature and at the age where he was emotionally and physically ready to have a wife. Paul tells us, "It is better to be married than to burn with desire" (1 Corinthians 7:9). So, Abraham sent his servant back to the land of Abraham's family in order to find a young virgin (morality was then as it should be today—important). Only a virgin would be considered worthy enough to be joined to a son and, of course, it was understood that the reason for the son getting married was so he would not lose his virginity until he was betrothed. Therefore, virginity was important for both men and women.

Even God demanded a virgin for His Son. In Isaiah 7:14, God tells the children of Israel that one day a virgin will conceive and have a child, and His name will be called Emmanuel. In Matthew 1:18 Mary conceives Jesus Christ through the Holy Spirit.

David acknowledged to the youth pastor that his love and respect for his mother could not even allow him to picture her being intimate with a man, much less sleeping around like he was doing. The youth pastor convinced David that since he respected his mother, he should respect the potential mother of his child. He explained to him that giving into sexual desires just because he was in puberty and showing the signs of manhood, did not make him a man. Self-control (godly behavior) is the hallmark of an adult.

We are oversimplifying the many months this pastor invested in this young man, but through the use of Scripture, he was able to help David develop a respect for the design God created in order to procreate the human race. God never intended sex to be filthy, but to be the joining of two souls into one. Although the youth pastor had no control over the dating habits of his youth group, it is always a good idea not to start dating until you are at least 17 and then date only in groups. In the Jewish Mishnah, having sex was a commitment of marriage under Jewish law. Regarding matrimony and the sexual joining of two people, Jesus refers to Genesis 2:24 when confronted by the Pharisees in the gospel of Matthew.

> The Pharisees also came unto Him, tempting Him, and saying unto Him, 'Is it lawful for a man to put away his wife for every cause?' And He answered and said unto them, 'Have ye not read, that He which made them at the beginning made them male and female,' And said, 'For this cause shall a man leave father and mother, and shall cleave to his wife: and they two shall be one flesh? Wherefore they are no more two, but one flesh. What therefore God hath joined together, let no man put asunder' (Matthew 19:3-6).

Through the union of a man and woman, as husband and wife, we too share in a manifestation of divinity as we are allowed the sacred honor of becoming initiators of life! The Holy Trinity foreshadows this type of union in a nonsexual way because we know there is only one God (Deuteronomy 6:4), and we know that God is manifested in three persons (Isaiah 48:16)[15]

It is not a very far stretch to think of a mother, a father and their child as being three separate individuals and joined together in a family unit that is similar to the Trinity of God. Of course, there are greater distinctions between God and man than the scenario the youth pastor used but the idea is there. A commitment of two people in a sexual union can result in the creation of a new life. This is as close to God that we as mere creatures can be. It is an awesome responsibility not to be taken lightly, because to live outside the design God has for our lives is to be serving the creature and the prince of darkness. Satan has young people believing that sex is fine, and many are taught in school, "As long as you are mature enough and really love the person ...." This is a lie, and the father of lies is Satan (John 8:44).

After almost a year of the youth pastor's investment of time with David regarding his promiscuous lifestyle, I am happy to say that David has repented, accepted the Lord and turned his life around. He enjoys dating in groups now because of the newfound respect he has for the girl he is dating. Before, dating was a sexual game.

To sum this up, David now has boundaries dictated and orchestrated through God's Word. He has restored his virginity as proof of his maturity until he is ultimately mature enough to consummate his love for a godly young woman on the night of his marriage.

NOTES:

1. I have encountered many people who consider themselves Christians, some based solely on the reason that they live in the United States. I call these people "social Christians" because their heredity is from a family of Christians and they feel they have inherited Christianity, not fully understanding that God does not have grandchildren. It is up to

your counselees to first understand that Christ paid a high price for their sins by offering His body as a blood sacrifice on Calvary's Cross. It is through His resurrection from the dead that your counselees have proof that Christ is truly God in human form. When they individually accept Him as their Savior, they no longer belong to themselves because He paid a high price for their souls. When they realize this, it then becomes their desire to please and live according to His moral guidelines, which are given for their benefit out of love and respect for their Savior.

2. ORTHO-NOVUM® Tablets and MODICON Tablets® Ortho-McNeil Pharmaceutical, Inc. Raritan, New Jersey 08869, oral contraceptive insert. Precautions: paragraph seven. "This is not exclusive to this specific product, but rather all contraceptives in general."

3. I have observed a new social phenomenon in recent years. Many couples dealing with a troubled conscience try to justify their sexual union by claiming the person they are sleeping with is their fiancé (man) or fiancée (woman). This seems to add a degree of legitimacy to their sexual relationship. However, nowhere in the Bible is sex permitted until it is blessed by marriage. Joseph and Mary were betrothed (engaged), but they did not engage in sex until they were married. "Now the birth of Jesus Christ was on this wise: when as His mother Mary was espoused to Joseph, before they came together, she was found with the child of the Holy Ghost. Then Joseph her husband, being a just man, and not willing to make her a public example, was minded to put her away quietly" (Matthew 1:18-19). In the Hebrew tradition, when a couple became engaged, they were (for all purposes) considered to be husband and wife. However, until the marriage ceremony was performed, they would not live together or have sex. The young man had to go to his father's house and prepare a room for the bridal couple. The potential groom did not know when he would be able to go and get his bride until his father told him he could. We see an example of this in Matthew 25:1-13.

4. *Random House Webster's College Dictionary* (1990), s.v. "self-esteem" (i.e., "self-respect"). However, as we demonstrated in chapter 1, the definition of "esteem" is to "regard highly"). When your counselees have good self-esteem, they have, in fact, a high regard for themselves. Another word for someone who regards himself highly is *conceit.* The Bible teaches that we should *esteem others* better than ourselves (Philippians 2:3). Remember that Jesus, who is God, washed His disciples' feet like a lowly slave (John 13:3-5).

5. Eleanor Ayer, *It's Okay to Say No: Choosing Sexual Abstinence* (New York: The Rosen Publishing Group, Inc., 1977), 13. Only 18% of unwed mothers receive any help from the fathers, even though the law requires him them to provide child support. This leaves 82% of unwed mothers virtually abandoned.

6. Because of their past reputations, we have many churches today which may seem like a good choice to a seeker who is "unchurched." The problem is that many old line denominations have fallen into heresy and deny the virgin birth as well as the resurrection of Jesus, along with many other misguided assumptions, including acceptance of *modern thinking* on the various unbiblical sexual relationships. Your counselees must either accept all that the Bible has to teach regarding sexual morals or completely dismiss everything that the Bible teaches. God's Word is not an ala carte menu, allowing the seeker to take what is appealing while rejecting what is not. It is a dangerous thing to be involved in an apostate church that manipulates the Word of God (Revelation 22:18-19).

7. In actuality, a Christian should never date an unbeliever and this includes "just a friend date." This is because after your counselees have gone out with someone once or twice, they should have summed up their date as a prospective marriage partner. If there are negatives, now is the time to break it off. Counselees should never go out with anyone, including friends, because their date should be their potential mate. With each instance of going out with someone, they are building bonds, and the bonds become stronger and tighter until it

becomes a cage that entraps them. The key to escape is no longer in their hands, but in the hands of the one with whom they have become involved. Counselees should be careful to realize there is no such thing as casual dating. Relationships are tentatively forever, and the commitment becomes very strong and real. They should be cautioned not to play with fire! I have known girls who make the excuse, "Well, I know he's not a Christian, but he's so cute that I can't help myself. Besides, I know I can change him." This is a cop-out. It is not that your counselees <u>cannot</u> help themselves; it is that they do not <u>want</u> to help themselves. "Missionary dating" does not work, and all too often the missionary winds up succumbing to the world.

8. We are dealing with *feelings*, self-gratification and a self-serving attitude. When your counselees allow themselves to sink into this emotional state, they are not able to serve Christ or put His needs (His desire for His children to have a Christ-edifying and fulfilling life) before their own. Question for your counselees: What is better to rely upon—their emotional *feelings* and perceived need for temporary stimulation, or an *eternal* plan of protection and blessing?

9. Sally does not like her lifestyle because her conscience is bothering her, and she wants to be a virgin again. First, through repentance she needs to get rid of her commitment to a promiscuous lifestyle, seek God's forgiveness and put on a new commitment to a pure lifestyle in Christ. Sally's only hope of changing is through Christ because through Him, the Bible assures her she can become a new creature (2 Corinthians 5:17).

10. 1 Corinthians 15:33-34 states, "Be not deceived: evil communications corrupt good manners. Awake to righteousness, and sin not; for some have not the knowledge of God: I speak this to your shame."

11. Gary Thomas, *Where True Love Waits: Sexual Abstinence Programs*, *Christianity Today* (March 1, 1999), 49. Susie is not alone. This happens all the time. Thomas relates a similar story told to him by Cathi Woods, counselor and founder

of a program who works with sexually-active teens in Rhea County, Tennessee. Woods tells of a girl who just turned 14 when she began dating. The boy she was dating kept pressuring her to engage in sex, and this young girl would seek advice on a few occasions from Woods. She bemoaned that the boy threatened to leave her if she would not give in and have sex with him. Woods tried to point out to the naïve teenager that what the boy wanted was not love. She kept encouraging the young teen to hold onto her virginity, which she did for several months. However, the day came when Woods received a disturbing phone call from the troubled teen, confessing that she had given into her boyfriend's demands a few weeks ago and now she was late for her period. Woods encouraged her to come into her office for a pregnancy test. Once the boyfriend found out the girl was pregnant, he left her. Sadly, upon examination by a doctor, the girl found out that not only was she pregnant, but her boyfriend had left her with incurable genital herpes. This young girl will be paying the consequences of her *feelings* for the rest of her life. Author's note: This young girl should also have been warned to drop this young man by pointing out that his actions proved that his intentions were no good.

12. David, a young man after God's own heart, truly loved God. He attempted in all his ways to lead a righteous life. However, like all of us, David had a sinful nature and lusted after a married woman. David could not contain his lust for her and used his good looks, authority and position to seduce her. David knew better, but instead of relying upon what he knew God had ordained for sexual relations outside of marriage, he chose to let his *feelings* control him. The lady's name was Bathsheba, and her husband, Uriah, was a loyal soldier in David's army. Because of a moment of passion, Bathsheba became pregnant. What was David going to do? He was a politician, the King. He had a great reputation and was famous for being a man of God. This moment of passion could undo all that for which David had spent his life working and fighting. We may ask, "Did David

biblically confess his sins to all concerned and ask forgiveness?" No, David reacted the way most of us would react; he tried to hide it. He listened to some bad advice and arranged for his loyal servant, Uriah, to be killed in battle (2 Samuel 11:15-18). As human beings, it seems we never learn that when we enter into sin and then try to use lies to cover up those sins, we make matters worse. Ultimately, the child of King David and Bathsheba died. In his heart, David was still a man of God who, like all of us at one time or another, had allowed himself to willingly sin. David called upon the Lord and confessed his sin. (Please read Psalm 51, which records David's repentant heart.) God forgave David for his sin, but because David had impregnated another man's wife and caused him to be killed, he had set into motion consequences of his actions that could not be undone. God assures David of his forgiveness but warns him (because he unjustly used the sword against Uriah), "Now therefore the sword shall never depart from Thine house; because Thou has despised Me and has taken the wife of Uriah the Hittite to be Thy wife" (2 Samuel 12:10).

13. Jay Adams, *The Christian Counselor's Manual* (Grand Rapids: Zondervan Publishing House, 1973), 172-173. Adams writes, "It is not the past that needs to be dealt with; actually the past no longer exists. It is not his past that needs changing; it is the counselee himself as he now is who must change."

14. Jack W. Hayford, Litt.d., General Editor *Spirit Filled Life Bible (NIV)* (Nashville: Thomas Nelson Publishers, 1991), 1888 (Heb 12:16, 17).

15. In Isaiah, we read an account of a member of the Trinity relating a story to us. We know the person speaking is Divine because He tells us He has existed from the beginning of time. He also speaks of God and the Holy Spirit. The Divine commentator in Isaiah states, "Come ye near unto me, hear ye this; I have not spoken in secret from the beginning; from the time that it was, there am I: and now the Lord God, and His Spirit, hath sent me" (Isaiah 48:16).

CHAPTER 6

STAYING A VIRGIN TEEN

DEALING WITH A GIRL'S FEELINGS

A SPECIAL MESSAGE FOR GIRLS

Shannon Sloane

For the benefit of your counselees who are young girls and approaching or have begun puberty, you may let them know there are female counselors, like me, who been there. Unlike guys when girls enter puberty drastic changes begin to affect their bodies. While some changes are not necessarily pleasant, such as having a menstrual cycle and abdominal and breast pains that accompany that cycle, girls' bodies also begin maturing from that of a child into a woman. At this point in your counselees' lives, confusion and frustration begins to challenge them. Many girls start growing taller than the guys in their class and their bodies start looking more like a woman. On the other hand, boys are still a little shorter, and their bodies do not show any radical changes toward manhood. With time, of course, both boys' and girls' bodies start looking more masculine and feminine. However, during the stage of life we are looking at now, those changes are more obvious with the girls.

This is also a time when the world starts putting lots of sexual pressures on them, and they notice that boys are also starting to notice them; not so much for whom they are anymore, but with the fascination of their breasts and developing shapes. While it is good for girls to remember that these changes are things everyone goes through and has to deal with, the passage from a little girl into a young woman is something that everyone goes through, including their mothers and grandmothers, it is important for you to share with them how they should celebrate becoming a young woman in God. They should cherish their virginity and keep themselves pure by recognizing the traps that Satan and the world have set for them.

During this age, girls' relationships with the guys in their classes start to change. Suddenly that geek, Bobby, changes overnight into that hunk, Robert. Girls experience new *feelings* that are sometimes confusing, but that is all part of growing up. It is what your counselees do with this gift of sexuality that God has given them that can affect their entire future and life, for better or worse.

Being a girl is fun. The passage from childhood and being a tomboy or Daddy's little girl to womanhood and a godly young lady can be fun and exciting times of their lives. As girls' interests change regarding such things as clothing, cars, boys and the prospects of one day getting married and/or having a career, they must set some very specific goals for their lives. Do not let this goal-setting scare your counselees. They do not have to make a list of strict rules that they must follow or never change because they are afraid of offending someone. They should not dread goal-setting either. Ultimately, God would not have given girls unreasonable rules that make them afraid to be who they are or be able to survive the passage of puberty. God does not want your counselees to be timid about their sexuality. One of His most precious gifts is the potential of one day becoming a mother. If God does not want them to marry and have families, He would not have given them those desires that lead them to be attracted to members of the opposite sex and the longing in their bodies for intimacy; the kind of intimacy that leads to creating a baby. Counselees have to be on guard about the way Satan has manipulated the world to exploit their God-given desires and pervert them into something that, if used outside of marriage, can cause unwanted consequences, heartbreak, disease, and even death.

Before and after girls enter puberty, many girls, including me, dream of one day having a handsome prince sweep us off of our feet, marry us, and carry us away to his castle where we would have children and live happily ever after. However, P.B. Wilson in her book, *Knight in Shining Armor*, cautions that once your handsome knight reaches down, grabs you by the waist and swings you up on the back of his charger (horse), you then see his back, and from behind he does not appear as handsome and impressive as he did from the front. She is telling us that we all have romantic dreams of a perfect future, but the truth is that even when we meet the most perfect man in the world, he will have his faults just as you and I have our faults.

This chapter is about how counselees can deal with their romantic desires. As girls grow older, some of the faults they might find in the guys they like can be guys trying to pressure them to go *all the way* with them, and one of the faults counselees might find in themselves is that they feel they have to have a guy to be somebody. Your female counselees must be careful. Girls are very different from boys, not only by their physical appearance, but in their *feelings* and the ways they see the world and people around them. God gave girls a nurturing soul, which means they are more attracted to guys who show them affection outside of physical touching, but we girls like to be held too. Girls are more interested in helping and encouraging those they really care about, and sex is not necessarily the driving force behind why they care for a guy. Girls tend to depend upon how they *feel* about people more than what they think about them. Sometimes girls *feel* they have to have a guy to be confident about themselves.

I have a friend who told me the same thing. She had to be in a relationship to *feel* fulfilled and loved. Perhaps it was because her father died before she was a teenager. Years later she met a guy she thought was the perfect man. She moved in with him and after a short period of time, he began physically abusing her, then turned around and bought her expensive gifts, promising her that he would never do it again. Things would be okay for awhile, and then he would abuse her even more and buy more gifts and make more promises. This became the pattern of their relationship. She *felt* good and secure that he was giving her all of these expensive gifts. He even gave her a car, but he kept the title in his name. Because they were living together like a married couple, she thought nothing about turning her paycheck over to him, but as this situation of abuse followed by gifts and more promises became continually worse and worse, she realized she was trapped in the relationship and could not escape. This guy cleverly deceived her. He took her money and replaced it with things. She had lots of "things," but no money to escape from him. In order to move from an unsafe situation to a place of sanctuary (safety and protection), down payments are required for a place to live and for utilities. Besides needing money to move, people also have to have good credit. A counselee should be glad that she is better off in her own home, and if she stays with her family she would not have to worry about those things. It would have been much better for my friend if she had stayed at home until a young man came along who loved and respected her so much that he would meet her mom, and spend time getting to know her. I do not mean through nighttime dating; I mean things like attending church with her and her mother, visiting museums, zoos, art shows, horseback riding or any type of event that includes daytime activities where other people are around.

One example for your counselee may be that if she has a one hundred dollar bill and she and her girlfriends were enjoying a day at the mall, would she take that one hundred dollar bill out of the security of her purse to put it on a counter and then walk away for a half hour and expect it to be there when she came back? The probabilities are very good that someone would have seen that hundred dollar bill and before she got a few steps away, grabbed it and spent it for something they wanted. This same thing is true of your counselee's virginity. If she carelessly flaunts it and leaves it out there for anyone to take, some guy will take her virginity and use it on something he wants. In this case, it would be him satisfying his own desires and not giving a second thought to what it costs her. So whether it is a hundred dollar bill or your counselee's virginity, she needs to be protective of it. She should not flash her money around;

likewise, she should not flash her sexuality around because it will attract the wrong kind of people. In the case of my friend, she was wise enough to finally realize that she needed to protect her morals and her body, so she returned to the safety of her mother's home and broke off the relationship with that guy. It is good for your counselee to keep in mind that if a guy prefers her with her clothes off and not with her clothes on, then he really does not want *her*.

When your counselee approached you with concerns about her lifestyle and the problems she is having, she did so because she was confused and curious about celibacy. Perhaps she is at a time in her life where lots of temptations and lifestyles are pulling at her from all different directions. Your counselee may be wondering, "Should I stay a virgin or not? What, if any, is all of the fuss about staying a virgin anyway?" One of the answers to the above questions is to share with your counselee some of the other chapters in this book or have her read the companion book, *You Can Be a Virgin Again*. Through this counseling, your counselee will be able to see how many young people and adults have regretted losing their virginity; so much so that they are seeking to help correct the wrong they had carelessly thrown away in a moment of lust. If they could start over again being a young girl such as your counselee and knowing what they know now about sex outside of marriage, they would. If your counselee could ask them why, they would tell her, "Staying a virgin may seem hard at times, but it is a lot easier to *stay a virgin* than trying to escape from a world of pressure to be sexually active and all of the problems it causes." Some of her *friends* will tell her that being pure is *old-fashioned*, yet there are only two options for your counselee. She either waits until she is married to have sex or she does not. Nothing is fashionably new. Your counselee only has two options. Those two options have been the same since the beginning of time and do not change or come in or go out of fashion. Only your counselee can eliminate one of the options; only she can choose what lies in store for her life. We are told today that a woman has the right to choose, and that is correct up to a point. The choice is to have sex or not, but all of the consequences of that choice come back to the first one, "Should I have given into sex before marriage or not?" If your counselee chooses to have sex before marriage, then the probability of her becoming pregnant and having to deal with that pregnancy becomes an issue. The taking of any human life at any stage has great consequences. Your counselee may think that to eliminate a "problem" now may not affect her life and it may not until years later, but young people, especially in their teenage years, do not usually think long-term and if they have a child out of wedlock, guys will know that they are sexually active and think they are an easier "score;" therefore, they will pursue them for their sexual gratification. Ask your counselee how many young men she thinks would want to commit themselves to supporting a wife and children when they can remain single and only have to support one—himself. We are not debating if these attitudes are right or wrong on the part of the guys, but only reflecting upon the realities of the world where we live. We do not live in a Christian world anymore. All you have to do is watch Nickelodeon with their toilet humor and sexual jokes aimed at children to realize that what used to be considered filthy are now just part of everyday television. The attitudes and morals of people have changed.

What is a girl to do? Girls have hormones too, and just like guys, when their hormones change, they start having reproductive urges. Saying "reproductive urges" may sound funny to young counselees because the world portrays sexual activity as a pleasure, fun, a great pastime, and a form of entertainment either by doing it or observing it through movies, television and the Internet. Yet, sex is really about *reproduction*. This is how the human race and all other living things maintain themselves on this planet. It would be safe to say that the primary purpose of sex, be it plants, animals or people, is simply to reproduce the species. However, the Creator of sex had planned for it to be something more, something very special that when a woman feels the embrace of her husband and the warmth of his body next to hers, she feels protected, loved and very special because it is the woman who makes it possible for a couple to become a family. It is the mother who is nurturing to her husband and their children. It is the mother who has traditionally been the heart of the home and if Jesus is living in her heart, it is the mother who is a blessing to the whole family, including her grandchildren and great grandchildren.

A shocking statistic with young people in high school having premarital sex reveals that on an average, their relationship will last 21 days after the couple engages in sex, and couples who sleep together before marriage results in divorce three times more than couples who waited to have sex until they were married.[1]

Pleasure is a gift from God, as is sex, but it is Satan who goes throughout the world perverting good things and turning those things into bad things; things that can even kill you (1 Peter 5:8). Young girls are bombarded by all kinds of media, from music to magazines, from "nonjudgmental" sex education in public schools to glamorized television commercials aimed directly at promoting an immoral lifestyle. One commercial depicts a lovely, liberated young woman shopping around a cosmopolitan city. The commercial is offering an over-the-counter product designed to stimulate her sex drive with the promise "... especially for women ... arouse your sexuality ... for you and your *relationship*." Most counselees are susceptible to what they see on television; if your counselee does not believe it, have her think about why a one minute commercial during the Super Bowl costs over a million dollars! Television is a powerful media that affects all of us and when it sends the wrong message, the results can be devastating and lives can be destroyed.

Your counselee may wonder how things that are promoted on television and feel good can be bad and even kill her, but there are some deadly diseases that can only be acquired through sexual activity. Some of your counselee's friends may tell her that it is okay to have oral sex (sodomy), but she can still contact sexual diseases such as herpes and AIDS this way. Once a person has AIDS, it is just a matter of time before they are prematurely dead. Who knows what other sexually transmitted diseases (STDs) may be out there that we have not discovered yet? A good example is AIDS. Not too long ago, it was rare for anyone to have heard of that disease.

Your counselee should be aware of a report published in 1994 by the Alan Guttmacher Institute. It warns, "Many teenagers, as well as adults, are indirectly exposed to more than one sex partner each year because their partner has had sex with someone else." According to the former U.S. Surgeon General, C. Everett Koop, M.D., "When you have sex with someone, you are having sex with everyone they have had sex with for the last 10 years, and everyone and their part-ners have had sex with for the past 10 years." As we showed in the chart at the end of chapter 2, if your counselee has had sex with one to two people she is actually exposed to three. If your counselee has had sex with three people, she is exposed to seven. If your counselee has had sex with six people, she has exposed herself to 63 people. Finally, if your counselee has had sex with a dozen people in the last 10 years, she has exposed herself to 4,095 people! What does your counselee think the chances are that one of those 4,095 people had a sexually transmitted disease, including HIV/AIDS, syphilis, gonor-rhea, chlamydia, herpes, etc.? Yet, if your counselee trusts in God and His design for a healthy sex life by keeping herself a virgin until she is married, she does not have to worry about exposing herself to the horrors of STDs.

Other statistics from the 1994 Alan Guttmacher Institute's publi-cation, *Sex and America's Teenagers* (pg. 39), states it is believed that over 12 million new sexual diseases are transmitted each year, two-thirds of which are among women and men under 25 years old, and that may possibly include your counselee's age group! With the world population having dramatically increased by millions upon millions more since 1994, the number of STD infections would be off the chart! To make matters even worse, teens are more prone to increased harm from sexually transmitted diseases because their antibodies are not as developed as those of adults.[2] However, the real reason your counselee should wait until she is married to have sex should not be motivated because she is afraid of hurting herself, but because she desires to please God. She needs to develop a personal relationship with Him. Your counselee must come to understand that she is God's very special girl, and He really wants to protect and love her. God wants her to grow closer to Him. We cannot repeat it enough. If she is not going to church now, as a Christian counselor, you really need to help her find a <u>Bible-believing</u> church. This means a church where you know without a doubt that you are wanted and loved, a church that is there to help and support you when you need help, and a church that is not afraid to call bad behavior what it is—sin, and is there to help and support her when she needs help.

My family has some old cookbooks; one of them that my mother and grandmother used was *Better Homes and Gardens New Cookbook*. One of the "*new cookbooks*" is over 50 years old and one is more recent. They both have the same title and they are both published by Meredith Press. The more recent of those two cookbooks that Mom bought 10 years ago is the 11th edition. This cookbook has some wonderful recipes, but imagine what would happen if we wanted to make waffles and the directions called for eggs, but we do not want to follow the directions because we want to experiment and make the waffles our own way and left out the eggs. The result would be a disaster. The eggs are needed to bind the flour and other ingredients together so our waffles would end up beautiful to look at and tasty as well.

Sex is the same way. God, who is the designer of the recipe for sex, has given us a recipe book (the Bible) that, like our family cookbooks, has many editions but the same excellent advice. God's recipe for sex is very clear on how to live a moral life, but if we decide we are going to ignore the instructions and do it our way, then we will ultimately wind up with a real mess. The good news is that whether or not we live in a Christian world, we are able to overcome temptations if we have Christ living in our hearts. However, as previously stated, your counselee must first love God and acknowledge that Jesus is her Lord and Savior before she can fight the enemy. "I can do all things through Christ which strengthens me" (Philippians 4:13, clarification ours). "For greater is He (Jesus) who is in me, than he (Satan) who is in the world" (1 John 4:4b, clarification ours).

Protecting your counselee's virginity begins at a very early age. As Christian counselors, we must caution parents to be very observant and careful about where their children are at all times. I remember when I was in a Christian elementary school and my class went to one of our fellow student's homes for a pool party. We were all having a wonderful time and then all of a sudden a boy came up and tried to pull off my bathing suit. To this day, I am embarrassed and disgusted thinking about that event. Some of the girls may have thought it was fun and daring, but I knew that it was ungodly, and I did not want any part of it. Decisions that we make in our lives regarding sex begin early, and counselees must be taught to always be on guard and to represent themselves as the daughters of Christ that they are. As girls get older, their bodies fill out more and their awareness changes from having boys as just friends to having boys being attracted to them; because of this they have to be more careful. Caution: Having boys as "just friends" can spell trouble. Your female counselees need to be reminded that boys think differently than girls do.

One of my dearest friends got involved in a really wonderful church that had and still has a great reputation, but unfortunately they had a married youth pastor who thought more of his own desires than those of being a godly man and husband. Without going into any great detail, my friend, who was a virgin at the time, went to bed with him. God's conviction weighed so heavily on her that to her credit, not only did she break up with this guy, she knew she had to restore her virginity and she did. I am not singling out churches and pastors to say that all pastors are like this because they are not.

I am reminded of a famous evangelist who would never be in a car with a woman by himself, other than his wife. If the rare occasion of an emergency would arise and he was the only one who could help, he would insist that the lady sit in the back seat so that there would not even be "the appearance of evil" (1 Thessalonians 5:22). Even though it is rare that a pastor would take advantage of his position with an innocent member of his congregation, as happened to my friend, counselees must still be on guard against situations that could lead them into a sinful situation.

As for my friend, I am happy to say that after she restored her virginity, she maintained it until she was married. Several years after that incident, she met a godly young man, fell in love and got married. She told me how shocked she was one time when they were alone together before they were married when he suddenly jumped up and abruptly left her sitting alone. She was wondering what she did wrong to cause him to leave her so quickly. She was quite hurt because she loved him and thought he loved her too. Then the phone rang. It was her boyfriend. He did love her. In fact, he loved her so much, in fact, that he confessed to her that when they were alone together he started having sexual desires toward her, and that was why he got up and ran out on her! That is a real commitment to God and a real commitment to the one you love. His respect for her was greater than his desire to try and satisfy his own needs. They now have a wonderful sexual relationship that has produced three beautiful children and a blessed and happy home.

As a former director for an inner city Crisis Pregnancy Center in the United States, I counseled many girls who allowed themselves to be involved with premarital sex. One of the problems that contributed to these girls being the object of sexual situations was the provocative way they dressed. Some of your counselees may think that just because the latest trends and department stores sell provocative (sexy) clothing does not mean that it is smart to dress that way. If girls lived in a world of just women, it really would not matter as much, but guys are very visual. True, girls want to be noticed by guys but in the right way. If your counselees dress like a whore by showing lots of skin, cleavage and their belly button, guys will expect them to behave like a whore. Counselees should not be in too big of a rush to date either. Most girls just like to be held, but to a guy that is the first step to even more intimacy. As I stated earlier, girls tend to be caught up in *feelings* and when they are with a guy they really like and think is cute, it becomes hard to say NO. Because of so much premarital sex in our nation today, whole industries have sprung up to deal with all of the babies that are conceived out of wedlock. Some organizations truly desire to help these young mothers deal with their pregnancies in a compassionate way. Other organizations, however, are happy to make a profit out of the unwanted predicament in which these young girls find themselves.

I know of a girl who had sex in high school with a guy she thought she would spend the rest of her life with. However, after giving herself to him, he grew tired of her and left her for someone else. She then met another guy who pressured her for sex and after giving into him, she soon found herself abandoned once more. She swore she would never give into a guy again. When asked what she got out of the affairs, she said she got nothing. I told her she was wrong. What she got out of those affairs was a distrust of men, deep pain and hurt, plus a sense of betrayal by being used, then tossed away. She also got something else out of those affairs—a loathing for sex as well as a bad image of herself and a sense of hopelessness and regret. She looked at me for a moment, nodded her head in agreement and then began sobbing. Do not fool yourself; sex outside of marriage is filled with hapless victims who say, "We're in love. That won't happen to us," only to have found themselves in my office, scared and facing an uncertain future. Many of the girls confessed that when they were late for their period, they would desperately pray to God for help. They promised Him that if they could start their period, they would never sin again only to forget that promise as soon as, although late, their period started again. God cannot bless your counselees if they are involved in a sexual relationship outside of marriage.

Many times I have heard, "But this is different, he really loves me and I really love him. God knows our hearts and love for each other. Besides, I feel something very spiritual when I am making love to my boyfriend." What a counselee is *feeling* may be spiritual; I have no doubt about that, but from which spirit world is it coming? Ask your counselee if she really believes that God would ask others to save themselves for marriage by promising that if they do, they will have unspeakable joy and happiness in their marital relations, but in your counselee's case, does she think God is willing to make an exception for her to have sex *before* marriage? As your counselee grows older and thinks she really loves someone, she needs to invest a few years getting to know him. Once he has shown that he loves and respects her by not pressuring her to sin against her own body and God, it would be good for them to get married. Getting married is a better option than allowing a situation to arise where your counselee and her boyfriend can no longer control their sexual desire for each other and give into those desires before they are married (1 Corinthians 7:9). As a Christian counselor, you know all too well that Satan will be whispering in your counselee's ear, "It's alright; God understands your needs. Besides, He made sex, and He knows how much you love each other. You're going to get married anyway, so what can it hurt? Go ahead, it's okay. No one will know." However, God will know and so will your counselee. I can tell you from personal experience that I almost gave into that same type of reasoning with a guy who said he wanted to marry me and told all of his friends we were getting married. I really believed him and allowed myself to be in a situation that almost cost me my virginity. I thank God that I did not allow myself to go any further and broke up with him soon afterward. I learned from that incident, and I have not allowed myself to be in any compromising situations again. I share this personal experience with you and your counselee so that your counselee will realize that sexual temptation can happen to anyone, and I hope that your counselee will be able to learn from my own situation. Counselees must be cautioned not let themselves get into situations that set them up for sex. In my case, it could have just as easily gone the other way, but because of the grace of God, it did not.

As a Christian counselor, you know that it is not just very young girls who get involved in sex. I am reminded of the time a young law student came into my office. She was involved with a young doctor and presumably, one of the reasons she was attracted to him was because he was compassionate, gentle and caring. His specialty was taking care of premature babies, helping them in their struggle to survive since they were born without the full capacity to live outside the womb on their own. She said she was pregnant and wanted to know what her options were as far as an abortion was concerned. I explained that abortion has been found to cause cancer in women and because she was an African-American, the risk of breast cancer was even higher for her. I further explained that there was a risk of death to the mother during the abortion process due to excessive bleeding and because the uterus is often damaged from the way abortions are performed, there was a possibility of not being able to get pregnant again. I also told her that after an abortion many women are not prepared for the unexpected post-abortion syndrome, which can include depression, anger and often the desire to commit suicide. I warned her that she might be able to undo her pregnancy through the termination of the baby's life, but she would never be able to undo the taking of that life once the abortion occurred. Knowing that her boyfriend specializes in saving fetuses and was involved in her pregnancy, I was curious as to what he thought. It was disappointing for me to learn that they had talked about it and he thought that since they were not married and she had not finished school, that it would be best for them if she had an abortion. They reasoned they could always have more children later. It was bewildering to me how her boyfriend could be so compassionate and skilled in saving lives of fetuses who found themselves unnaturally outside the womb, while never giving a second thought to killing a fetus who was still inside its mother's womb, especially when this fetus was his own child. I seriously doubted that this man was really as compassionate and caring as he appeared to be.

Because this chapter is for the benefit of your young counselees who are still virgins, but rapidly approaching how to deal with the sexual changes that are happening in their bodies, I tried to show through the above incidents that not all is what it seems. Just because a guy may be connected with a church, or a doctor who tries to save the lives of babies, or a man who has promised he is going to marry you, does not mean that your counselee can let her guard down. In each of the above cases, including my very own story, I have tried to show that your counselee needs to be very careful about who she trusts and in what situations she allows herself to be in with them. Many young girls do not always think past what they are going to wear, what they are going to buy at the mall this weekend or all of the latest news about their girlfriends and their boyfriends. I know some people would say this level of maturity is just being childish, but the truth is that when I was 11, 12 and in my early teens, I was a kid. I had fun being a kid. It is one of the most fun times of our lives if we do not mess it up. So while your counselee may be trying to hurry and grow up, she should be cautioned to step back and think for a moment that being a kid is not really so bad, but being a kid who *has* a kid destroys her childhood. God understands this, and He wants all of us to stay virgins until we are mature enough to be in a committed relationship of marriage. Just because girls' bodies start developing and they start having their periods does not mean that they are emotionally mature enough to get married, and if they are not old enough to get married, the wise thing to do is follow God's advice and save themselves until they are old enough for a godly relationship with the husband He has for them.

There is another story about a beautiful young girl who kept herself pure and virgin before God and her community. She was from an ethnic minority in the country where she lived, and there was a lot of prejudice and hostility toward her people. Many people in America can relate to how hard it is when you are an immigrant. It takes many generations before people are either absorbed or accepted as a group in their new country. This beautiful young girl had the opportunity to meet the head of her country who, in her society, was the king. The king was looking for a wife, but he was very particular and wanted only the best woman to become his queen. Because of her commitment to keep herself pure before God, not only was this girl outwardly beautiful, but inwardly beautiful as well. The king fell madly in love with her and asked her to be his bride. To make a long story short, as queen, she was able to help her people overcome the hostility and hatred that others had felt toward them for so long. Her name was Esther and if your counselees would like to find out more about her, they can read her story in the Bible in the book named after her.

Restored virgins are also found in the Bible. It would be good for us to revisit the story of Naomi and her daughters-in-law (previous mentioned in chapter 4) and see another aspect that God had in mind for Naomi's daughter-in-law, Ruth. As a biblical counselor, you may recall how Naomi's family had to leave their country and move to another because of a great famine. She had two fine sons who married two lovely local girls. Unfortunately, just when everything seemed to be going well, her husband died and so did her sons. Enough time had gone by that the famine in her homeland had ended. With her husband and sons gone, she did not have any reason to stay in this foreign country any longer and decided to return home. She told her daughters-in-law that although she loved them, it would be best for them to stay in their country because they were still young and could remarry. At this point, the story changes for Ruth who commits to living the life of a restored virgin. Ruth made the decision to return to Naomi's homeland with her. Ruth remained a faithful daughter-in-law and after awhile, God honored her commitment to her mother-in-law and to Him (she accepted Naomi's God as her own) and rewarded her with a fine husband who was kind, loving and wealthy. This marriage never would have been possible if she had not lived a virtuous virgin lifestyle. However, this is not the end of the story. Because of Ruth's commitment to her virginity before she was married and after she became a widow, and because of her godly devotion to her mother-in-law and new husband, God gave her a very special grandson named Yeshua or as we know Him, Jesus. Your counselees can read about this story in the book of Ruth in the Bible.

As we see from the stories in the Bible, God honored these women for honoring Him. He made one a queen and the other the grandmother of the Messiah. Counselees should appreciate that God gives them these stories to encourage them toward maintaining their virginity so they may enjoy a higher quality of life and a brighter future. He gives all of us the hope for a good life, not by scaring us so that we will be good, but by promising us that He loves us so much and assuring us we are very special to Him. He wants that same special relationship to be shared with your counselee's future husband too. By accepting Jesus as their Lord and receiving the eternal gift of life for the price that He paid for all of us on the Cross, your counselees are assured that He only wants the very best for them and God's best is far better than anything Satan has to offer. The wages of sin is death (Romans 6:23a).

I love being a girl. I love the wonderful life God has allowed me to live and the friends He has sent my way. I am proud that I am still a virgin and would never have it any other way. I know that God is preparing a husband for me and me for him. I look forward to the day he takes me in his arms and asks me to marry him. Until that day, however, I plan to honor God and His plan for my life. If it is not God's will for me to marry, I will still honor Him and remain faithful to Him by remaining a virgin and living a chaste Christ-honoring life. Like you, I really care about your counselees and pray that they will care about themselves too. As Christians, we are part of God's elect (Isaiah 45:4; 2 Timothy 2:10), and are grafted into His elect, Israel (Romans 11:17-18). We, therefore, benefit from all of the blessings God has promised to His people.

For I know the plans I have for you, declares the LORD, plans to prosper you and not to harm you, plans to give you hope and a future (Jeremiah 29:11, NIV).

Who can find a virtuous woman? For her price is far above rubies (Proverbs 31:10).

Favor is deceitful, and beauty is vain: but a woman that fears (respects) the LORD, she shall be praised (Proverbs 31:30, clarification ours).

NOTES:
1. J.D. Teachman, J. Thomas, and K. Paasch, "Legal Status and the Stability of Coresidential Unions," *Demography*, November 1991, 571-83. As quoted in *Good News About Sex and Marriage*, p. 71.
2. *Is Sex Safe? A Look at: Sexually Transmitted Diseases* (Lewiston: Life Cycle Books, 1998).

CHAPTER 7

STAYING A VIRGIN TEEN
GUYS HAVE FEELINGS TOO
A SPECIAL MESSAGE FOR GUYS

J.P. Sloane

If anyone had to struggle with temptation growing up, it was me. I was born in Hollywood, California. My parents had their own shows on radio and television. As a result, I began singing at three years old and performed on radio, television and in motion pictures. I was featured on the cover of comic books that were distributed worldwide. I recorded my first record when I was a teenager. I am sharing this with you to let you know that I was exposed to all sorts of temptations that most kids only dreamed of back then. I can tell you that I made many wrong and sinful decisions that I am truly sorry for and still regret to this day. So please believe what I am about to tell you and your counselees because I am speaking from experience when I warn that what may seem cool and glamorous on the surface is really a demonic trap set to catch your counselees and ruin their lives. In spite of the fact that I was exposed to a lot of sin while I was growing up in the entertainment industry, your counselees live in a society that would have been unheard of for the average teen when I was their age. However, this does not mean that your counselees cannot rise above the temptation and evil that has become common place in today's world. When I was a child, I had some very famous people put me on their knee and reflect upon the times in which we lived. They would say something like, "I know you won't listen, but ..." and then continued to give me their advice. I did not like being told that I would not listen so I did! I listened to everything they told me, and to this very day I still draw upon the wonderful lessons of life they taught me. As young men, I hope your counselees will also take to heart what I am about to share with you and them.

To begin with, there is a true story about a young man who, probably like your counselee, was dealing with puberty. As Christian counselors, you know puberty lasts for several years, although the urges produced by those hormones continue to affect us all for the rest of our lives. It is how your counselee handles these urges from the very beginning that will affect how he will deal with them as a teenager, a young man, a faithful and godly husband and father. This particular guy was 17 years old and had been dealing with his sexual urges for several years. The hormonal changes that occurred over the past few years changed his appearance too. No longer was he a lanky little boy; he had filled out into a muscular and handsome teenager. Due to some unfortunate events this young man got into when he was younger, he found himself in an unusual predicament. The good thing was that his life was beginning to straighten out; he had a great job with a powerful politician. This politician had a beautiful but unfaithful wife. Some women find politicians particularly attractive because of the power and money they have. However, any woman who would be ambitious enough to take advantage of their beauty in order to get a rich and powerful husband they did not love is not someone you could respect.

So it happened that our handsome young teenager, who I will refer to as Joe, became an object of this married woman's sexual desire. Joe was a decent young man in spite of the fact that he was a rather spoiled kid. He loved God and wanted to do a really good job for his boss, but he did not know that his employer's wife was thinking about how she could lure him into bed. She knew that older boys and 17-year-old guys were dealing with raging hormones, and she figured it would not take much to "turn him on." Because she was very street-wise regarding sex and knew how to excite guys, she planned a little trap for Joe. She waited until her husband was out of town on business, dressed really sexy and called for Joe who was out by the pool. When he came to her room, she quickly made her move. The lights were low, and she had tight fitting clothes on that really showed off her body. He must have been thinking, "Boy, this chick really knows how to get a guy!" At first Joe did not realize what was going on, but soon he knew she was out to get him. Joe was no different than most men. Seeing a really sexy girl who knew how to put the moves on him got his blood stirring and his head spinning. Joe must have been thinking, "Man, she is hot!" I know that I would have been stunned for a moment too wondering what to do; but Joe did not say something like, "You're really tempting me, but you know this is wrong. Let me tell you about Jesus. He says that to look at a woman with lust is committing adultery. You see ma'am, the Bible says …." No, that is not what he did. While you and I may think that would be a good opportunity to witness to her, Joe knew better. He started to run from her. She was mad! She reached out and grabbed hold of Joe's swimming trunks and with one fast pull yanked them clean off of him. He never looked back but kept on running. Then she started screaming, "Rape, rape!" "Somebody help me!" Soon everybody who was within hearing distance came running. She was so ticked off at Joe for refusing to have sex with her that she was going to get even and get even she did. She called the police, showed them Joe's swimming trunks, and had some of the other servants tell the police that they heard their bosses' wife screaming rape and saw a naked guy named Joe running from her bedroom. Joe was hauled off to jail on attempted rape charges. It was his word against hers and remember, her husband was a powerful and respected politician, and Joe was just a kid.

It would be nice if the world we live in was good and justice was always fair, but this is not the case. Poor Joe was convicted of attempted rape and sent to jail where he remained for several years. Can you imagine how Satan must have tormented Joe all of those years he was in jail saying things like, "Well Joe, you're still a virgin, but what did that get ya? If you would have partied with your bosses' ol' lady, you would have had lots of good sex and nobody would have been any smarter; but stupid, you had to run away and now you're in jail! Boy, are you dumb or what?" When Joe finally got out, he did not seek revenge or say, "To heck with being a virgin. It didn't get me anywhere. I'm going to go out and get me a girl and make up for lost time." No, Joe kept his virginity and remained a godly young man. Not by anything he said, but more importantly by how he acted. After awhile, all who knew Joe realized he would never try to hurt, much less rape anyone.

God also knew about the terrible temptation and suffering that Joe went through. Joe did not live in the United States of America but in a Kingdom in Africa. Because of Joe's honesty and godly life, even in the face of false arrest and imprisonment, it became obvious to all that here was a very special young man. God honored Joe's commitment to Him and to his virginity. Because Joe did not give into his sexual temptation and remained a virgin, God rewarded him with a very special wife from one of the most respected families in the kingdom, and the King himself made Joe his Prime Minister. Joe had it made. This is a true story and your counselees can read about this part of Joseph's life in Genesis, chapters 39-41.

Sex is a very powerful and desirable thing to be enjoyed. God made it, but your counselee must keep his emotions under control. If your counselee can do that, then he will be showing signs of becoming a *real* adult. As every biblical counselor knows, God designed it and He knows how it works best. Because of that, not only does He want the best for your counselee, He also wants your counselee to offer only the best to his future bride!

As I explained earlier, my family was in the entertainment business which exposed me to many temptations as a child. My dad told me that I would be offered drugs, but that I should not mess with them. This is another one of those "… but you probably won't listen to me …" things I told you about that I heard from adults when I was a kid. I did listen. My dad wisely told me, "Why start something you don't miss now but if you try, it may control you and ruin your life? Why take that chance?" That made a lot of sense to me. If I don't miss something I never had, then why take the chance of becoming addicted by trying it? You cannot be caught by something if you do not get near it.

At the age of your young counselee, most in his age group do not think a lot about the future. I did not either when I was his age. I thought mostly about girls. If a girl had a pretty face, I was in love. I never realized that in a few years she could gain weight, get wrinkled or her taste in men might change and she would no longer like me. All that mattered was that I was interested in her at that time. The longest I ever looked into the future was my next birthday, Christmas or summer vacation. I never gave much serious thought as to what I might be when I grew up or what kind of person I would want to marry. I figured those things would take care of themselves. All I knew was that she had to be cute so the other guys would be impressed. I never thought about what I wanted in a girl beyond her pretty face. I never thought what I would like in her as far as education, politics or religion. I never thought about what type of career she would want, whether she would want to be a stay-at-home mom (which is a full-time job in itself) or have a career outside of the home; if so, what type of career, how many children we would have, where we would live and how we would pay for it. I never thought about higher education other than graduating and escaping from high school. The list may be different for your counselee, but whether it was me then or your counselee today, these are things that a mature person must consider. We must continually remind our young men that sex outside of marriage can ruin it all.

Today, the focus is on high self-esteem. Everywhere I look, all I see are people, young and old, who are filled with self-esteem. Even those who are angry because they are unable to attain what they want and beat up others to get what they want are filled with self-esteem. "How can that be?" Many may argue, "People who are being bad are just 'acting out' their frustration at society for treating them poorly." What really lies at the root of such uncivil behavior? People act out in a bad way because they really do think highly of themselves; so highly, in fact, that they think others owe them, so they take what they want. Because they think so highly of themselves, they cannot say no to themselves. Another way of putting it is that they esteem themselves so highly that they cannot refuse themselves anything, and that includes sex! Think about it. Everyone is told that they are a victim. If a guy gets a girl pregnant, he is not told he sinned against her and his body and God. Instead, he is told it is the girl's fault, or that he should be more careful the next time. Girls look at sex differently than men, especially when guys are young and just beginning to have sexual urges. God made girls to be nurturing, loving and desiring to please those they care about. Girls are more in tune with personalities and relationships. Guys are visual and self-centered. Guys are more interested in instant gratification and then move on to something or someone else. "Been there, done that," so the saying goes. If there is no one to guide your counselee, he can cause himself trouble — casual sex outside of marriage can, *and will*, reach far into his future. The mistakes counselees make while growing up, especially sinful ones, can haunt them later in life. Because young people usually do not think that far ahead, your counselee may doom himself to suffer for things he may not be aware of as being sinful. Without biblical counseling, he may not realize that what he is doing is sinful until he is older and wiser, but by then it will be too late to undue it all. I know; I did some things when I was young that I am sorry for now, but it is too late to do anything about it now. Please do not let your counselee confuse God's grace (an undeserved gift) as something he can count on if he decides to have sex now and ask for forgiveness later because God is smarter than that. While it is true that God can forgive your counselee later if he *really* has a repentant heart, it does not mean that the consequences of his actions will disappear too.

Help him to stop and think about this: He may think that because he is in a youth group at his church, or goes to church on most Sundays and really loves God that he does not need to be too concerned about falling into sexual sin. As biblical counselors, we know that is exactly when Satan is most likely to slip one over on your counselee. He sneaks up on us when we least expect it.

Here is another true example about a young man named Dave. He volunteered for military service at a very young age. In fact, he was so young that his dad had to okay it. He was like some of your counselees; he studied the Bible and went to church services regularly. Dave was a very brave and handsome young guy who loved God with all of his heart. He remained a virgin until the day he was married and everyone admired him as a man of God. Dave rose through the ranks of the military and became the commander of all the armed forces. There came a time when his country was at war. However, because of Dave's high position, he was needed more at work than on the front lines of battle. One day, while Dave was taking a break from his responsibilities in his "high-rise building," he spotted a lovely woman across the way stepping out of her bath. I do not know why he was acting like a peeping Tom, but his whole life changed with what happened next. He arranged to have some of his friends introduce him to her. Then he used his good looks and position that God had given him to seduce this lovely woman who happened to be married to one of his acquaintances. It is not surprising that when you have sex you have babies, which is what happened with Dave and this woman. To make matters worse, he panicked and forgot everything he read in the Bible and learned in church. All he could think of was getting out of a terrible situation, a situation of his own making! Because he was in charge of the military, he arranged for one of his officers to have this woman's husband relocated to the front lines and gave orders to have the other soldiers quickly pull back, leaving her husband surrounded by the enemy where he knew they would be sure to kill him. Dave was sure this would solve his problem, but it did not. Guilt hounded him day and night and soon a son was born to Dave and the recently widowed woman. After awhile the child became ill, so Dave cried out to God for forgiveness and mercy on his illegitimate son. God heard his prayers and while He forgave Dave, He did not spare the child's life. As a result, Dave found out that you cannot take God for granted. What you plant is what you get. When your counselees plant things that please their sinful lusts, they too can be hurt by the things they produce.

This guy was so crushed by his sinful actions, especially because he was raised in church and knew better. After it was all over with, he threw himself on God's mercy begging Him for forgiveness; but all of the pain and allowing himself to become involved in an even worse sin in order to cover up his sexual sin could have all been prevented. How? He should not have allowed himself to sin by looking at someone who brought out his sexual desire and engaging in something that he should not have been doing in the first place. He complicated the matter by acting out that sexual desire. One sin leads to another, then another and still another until we are trapped in a cycle of sin from which we cannot free ourselves. This story is true. It is about King David, who was a man after God's own heart. Your counselees may read about it in the Bible, 2 Samuel 11. (You may also reference Note number 12 at the end of chapter 5.) This story is a good testimony of how your counselees may be godly people and think they are safe in God's will, but they must be doubly careful because this is the time that Satan will use to *blindside them*!

Finally, we must deal with the subject of masturbation. Some counselees think this is a good way to release sexual tension and keep themselves virgins, but they must be careful because they are playing with fire. The more your counselees give into their body's desire for food, cigarettes, alcohol, drugs or sex, the more they open themselves up to becoming addicted. We have to have food, but the other things we can avoid. Our minds have us believing that "just once won't hurt," but the just once only serves to wet (stimulate) our body's appetite for more. We cannot become an alcoholic (drunkard) unless we take our first drink or become addicted to drugs if we do not try them. We cannot become involved in a sexual lifestyle if we are smart enough to avoid sex outside of marriage. The truth is that our body is never satisfied and once it is exposed to something habit-forming, it soon gets the upper hand. We then become slaves to those desires the Bible calls lusts.

When I was 12 years old, I sneaked some cigarettes and thought I looked really cool. When I turned 30, I was smoking a cigarette and puffing on my asthma inhaler. I would take another drag on the cigarette and another puff on my inhaler. Suddenly it dawned on me. "This is stupid! Why am I smoking this stuff? My lungs are starting to shut down on me, and I'm abusing my asthma medicine." Finally, I wised up, repented before God and begged for Him to save me from my slavery to cigarettes. I am glad to say God delivered me. I will not lie to you, however; I admit that I failed a few times, but almost from the time of my prayer, I was able to stop smoking, and I have not smoked for over 25 years!

A very good friend of ours, Dr. Frank Wilson, explains that the lust of your flesh is like keeping a beast in the basement. Once you let it out, it wants to be fed. Once you feed it, it wants more. Its appetite is so ravenous that you can never satisfy it, and in the end the beast will devour you!

When your counselee masturbates, what does he fantasize about? Is it that cute girl he has been drooling over from a safe distance? That is sinful, and the Bible calls it lust because your counselee is having virtual sex with her in his mind. If the opportunity would arise, the probabilities are good that he could not stop himself from having a real sexual encounter with her, and that would allow the beast your counselee let out of the basement to not only destroy his virginity and cause this girl to sin, but it would also let the beast rob the girl God has chosen for him one day to be his wife and the mother of his children. The beast will also devour the innocent security of your counselee's children because they will find out they have a dad who sinned against God and their mother before he married her. They may also think that sex outside of marriage is okay because "dad did it." A fantasy life can lead your counselee into pornography which could pull him into an evil act that he may never have thought about before he exposed his mind to that filth.

As with drugs, why begin playing around with something that will ultimately take control of our bodies and minds as well as putting our souls in jeopardy of eternal Hell? Sadly, many young men are able to relate to masturbation and sexual fantasy, but are unable to think past the temporary pleasure to the long-term problems and suffering that can develop. Ask your counselee if it is really worth a minute or two of pleasure in exchange for a lifetime of regret? If he is able to recognize the danger, he will have no problem avoiding it. However, because he is young and does not have the wisdom and experiences that older men should have, he can easily be tricked. "If it looks good and it *feels* good, do it," we are told, but that is exactly what the unsuspecting fish thinks when it sees a big, fat, juicy worm dangling helplessly in front of it. If the fish is offered only a sharp hook, he would be smart enough to swim away, but that tasty worm on the hook is so tempting that he cannot refuse it. Perhaps he nibbles it "just to see," but that first taste around the edges triggers his lustful desire to satisfy his cravings for a juicy tidbit, so he goes for it "hook, line and sinker!" The fish gave into its lust, and it cost him dearly.

There is a famous story about a guy who wanted to satisfy a bodily urge; in his case (just like the fish), it was a desire for some fast food. Without thinking, he threw away his only inheritance because he craved some fast food! He was only thinking of satisfying his body's immediate cravings. Once his stomach was full and the urge had passed, he regretted what he had done; however, it was too late, and now someone else had his inheritance. For a moment of lust, he lost a fortune. He should have thought about that *before* he made the trade of his inheritance for a bowl of soup, but he did not. If anyone would have warned him, he probably would not have listened. He was only looking for pleasure and living for the moment.

How about your counselees? Are they mature and grounded enough in the Bible to avoid the kind of trouble that a moment of sex can bring? Can they pass up something that seems like fun and feels good for a short time in exchange for how it may affect the rest of their life? The story I have just told can be found in the Bible in the book of Genesis 25:29-34 and chapter 27.

Every man was once a teenager, and there is nothing new that your counselee has to deal with that other grown men have not had to go through. It does not stop there either. Just like your counselee, we too are being tempted everyday by the very same media and its sexually-charged advertising and programming that your counselee is exposed to and, like your counselee, we must also deal with it. It is also important for your counselee to remember that even though he may be young and still in school, he is still held accountable for his actions. God gave him (and all young males) the sexual identity of a man and the hormones that go with it. He has the potential to father children and affect the lives not only of himself, but the girl, her parents, his parents and any children they may have. They all have a right to hold your counselee accountable for his actions. He should not be allowed to blame his sinful actions on the girl. It requires two to create a baby. More importantly, God will hold your counselee accountable for his actions and being a pre-teen or a teenager does not excuse him. When God gives us something that is precious, and the gift of sex is precious, He will hold us accountable for how we use that wonderful gift. So encourage him to protect his mind as well as his body, and guard himself against sexual misconduct. Caution him against that old lie which states, "It's okay to experiment; everyone does it." He should avoid any experience that could turn a blessing from God into a demonic curse. One of the best defenses to protect your counselee from getting into sexual situations is for him to avoid them. Some simple ground rules will help him avoid trouble. He should not date until he is at least 17, and then do it only in groups. When he gets older and begins to think about marriage, that is the time for serious dating. He should be advised to only date someone he would consider as a potential mate. He should be warned to never kiss a girl when he is alone with her because that can start "a chemical reaction" that can bubble over in no time at all, and if he does kiss her, he should do it only on the cheek. He would be wise to keep a safe distance. It may sound old-fashioned, but holding hands can mean more between couples that are really attracted to each other than heated passion, which can leave them confused and out of control. A *real* kiss should be experienced by a couple only on their wedding day; they should save themselves for what should be a wonderful wedding night.

Statistics show that couples who are virgins and never live together before marriage have a high rate of success compared to those who "mess around" before marriage. Couples who have sex before marriage and/or live together first before marriage will almost always end in divorce![1] If your counselees are like I was at their age, they do not really care about statistics, but are more interested in sex. Once your counselee starts maturing sexually, he has to be able to handle that responsibly; if not, he will have to deal with even bigger problems that he will wish he could ignore, but will not be able to do so. If he does not deal with the problems before they happen, he *will* have to deal with the consequences. A good way for him to interact socially with a girl is to get to know her, then go to some shared events where there are a lot of people. He should meet her parents, brothers and sisters.

Finally, regarding waiting until the wedding night to have sex for the first time, let your counselee consider this similar occasion. Have him imagine that he has a favorite skateboard he loves, or maybe he will not have to pretend because he really does love his skateboard. He uses it almost everyday, and after three years of owning it, he would not trade it for anything. Let him imagine that today is his birthday and the anticipation and excitement are building because in an hour he is having a big birthday bash, and his parents have a special gift for him. The big moment has arrived, and his father hands him a beautifully wrapped gift. With the excitement and adrenalin rush in his trembling fingers, he struggles to open the package. He has been waiting with great expectation for weeks, and finally the moment arrives. He tears the paper from the box and is about to lift the box top from the package. He takes a deep breath and lifts the top off of the box exposing—his same old favorite skateboard. Now he still loves his skateboard, but getting something he already has is definitely not a very exciting birthday present. If your counselee has sex before marriage, it is just recycling the same old thing on his wedding night. Getting his old skateboard for his birthday is not very special, nor is having sex on his wedding night special either because it's old stuff. God has many reasons for keeping all of us virgins until marriage, and this is one of them. Our honeymoon should be exciting, special and new. If he stays a virgin, his wedding night will become a point in time that they both will remember and cherish together for the rest of their lives; God will honor and bless your marriage because you honored Him by waiting.

It is good to reinforce to your counselee that it all begins in the mind. The thought must precede the action, so he must defend his mind from those thoughts that can lead him into trouble. Have him use the Scriptures we have included for men at the end of chapter 10 for homework so that when his thoughts begin drifting into sexual lustful thoughts (and it will), he can begin redirecting his thoughts on some of those Scriptures. When a counselee gets into this habit, it will help get his mind off that which can cause him to indulge himself in sinful lusts and refocus his desires toward pleasing God. If he leads a life that is pleasing to God, he will be able to look back over his life and realize it was much better than the lives of some of his friends who liked to "party" and "have fun" by drinking and having sex. Your counselee will be able to look upon their lives which will probably be full of problems; failed relationships, divorce and even drunkenness, while his life will be satisfying, rewarding and fulfilled with a minimum amount of problems. I am not saying that there will not be bumps and challenges along the way; we all have times of trials, but your counselee can be assured that God will be with him and help him to get through them.

To think that we are able to address many of the problems of puberty in this short chapter would be foolish; however, this short chapter will give you and your counselee something to think about.

Christian counselors understand that biblically there are many reasons why your counselees should avoid becoming preoccupied and involved with sex outside of marriage. It can lead to not only unwanted pregnancies, but to untreatable diseases that can cause permanent and reoccurring infections, some of which will even cause them to die. (Refer to the risk chart in chapter 2 of this book.) However, as a Christian young man, the motivation to be pure should be his earnest desire to please God. More importantly, the girl he will marry and his very own children will thank him for being a godly husband and daddy; he will be thankful too!

My son, if you will receive My words, and hide My command-ments with you; So that you incline your ear unto wisdom, and apply your heart to understanding; Yes, if you cry after knowledge, and lift up your voice for understanding; If you seek her (wisdom) as silver, and search for her as for hidden treasures; Then shall you understand the fear of the LORD, and find the knowledge of God. For the LORD gives wisdom: out of His mouth comes knowledge and under-standing. He lays up sound wisdom for the righteous: He is a buckler (shield) to them that walk uprightly. He keeps the paths of judgment, and preserves the way of his saints (*all* who accept Jesus as their Lord and Savior). Then shall you understand righteousness, and judgment, and equity; yes, every good path (that you should take). When wisdom enters into your heart, and knowledge is pleasant to your soul; Discretion (caution) shall preserve you, understanding shall keep you: To deliver you from the way of the evil man, from the man that speaks *wicked*[2] things; Who leave the paths of uprightness, to walk in the ways of darkness; Who rejoice to do evil, and delight in the *wickedness* of the wicked; Whose ways are crooked, and they *do wicked* in their paths: To deliver you from the strange woman, even from the stranger which flatters (you) with her (sexually enticing) words; Which forsakes the guide (instruction) of her youth, and forgets the covenant of her God. For her house inclines unto death, and her paths unto the dead. None that go unto her (have sex with her) return again (to a chaste, virgin life), neither take they hold of the paths of life. That you may walk in the way of good men, and keep the paths of the righteous. For the upright shall dwell in the land, and the perfect shall remain in it. But the wicked (sexually immoral) shall be cut off from the earth, and the transgressors shall be rooted out of it (Proverbs 2, clarification ours).

NOTES:

1. .Research Alert, *Future Vision* (Naperville, Ill: Source-books Trade, 1991), 43. The chances of a marriage lasting among couples who live together before marriage have an 80% greater chance of divorce than individuals in a traditional marriage.
2. Forward and forwardness in the King's English of 1610 trans-lates into wicked and wickedness in today's English.

CHAPTER 8

A MAN CAN BECOME A VIRGIN AGAIN TOO!

J.P. Sloane

How can a young man keep his way pure?
By living according to Your Word.
I will seek You with all my heart;
Do not let me stray from Your commands.
I have hidden Your Word in my heart
That I may not sin against You
(Psalm 119:9-11, NIV).

This text, while containing material presented in a manner that helps men relate to the complex sexual issues they face, it is by no means directed only to men. Every chapter holds vital material, based upon God's Word, which is equally applicable to both men and women. If your counselees have our companion book, *You Can Be a Virgin Again*, it would be advisable to have them read *all* of the material in that book in order for them to fully understand the complexities of the plan God has for all of us as sexual beings.

In most cultures, throughout history, there has been a *male mystique*, which implies that a man's virility or manhood is expressed by the number of women he could sexually "conquer" or "seduce." With women demanding equal rights today, they have become sexual aggressors as well. As we previously discussed in this book, people and even more specifically men, are continually bombarded by sexual stimuli. Scantily dressed porn stars do sexual gyrations just to sell hamburgers. In today's economy with today's technology it becomes not only possible, but also probable, to equate fast sex with fast food.

Realizing that television has become an area where the envelope of indecency is pushed further and further, each season many broadcasters include soft and hard pornography, but try to pacify concerned family subscribers by offering them cable boxes that have *parental controls*. While the media will not give up their lucrative money-making "adult programming," they believe that such options as parental controls will keep those of us appeased who are offended by the use of our Lord's name in vain and programs that offer gratuitous sex and violence. This may be fine for R-rated programs, but what about commercials? In one hour of viewing television during the early afternoon, when children were out of school for summer vacation, we witnessed five commercials selling cures for male enhancement and erectile dysfunction. Some of these ads were promoted by a man with a silly grin plastered on his face in a commercial that was made to appear as if it were one of those *safe* 1950s commercials. Other commercials show a very attractive young woman who was also satisfied by her partner's performance while using one of these drugs. (Unfortunately, the words *partner* and *significant other* are widely acceptable secular and politically correct terms that have replaced not only the word *spouse*. Several of these sex-enhancing drug ads even warn, "If you have an erection more than four hours, seek medical help immediately." Not to be left out, there are now equivalent drugs offered to stimulate the female libido (sex drive)! Just imagine what mommy is going to tell little Johnny when he asks what a male erection is or how she is going to explain to little Suzie why a girl would want to have an active libido!

Take a closer look at what is called "adult entertainment." Think about it. When we are children, we cannot wait to grow up. We see adults smoking, so we want to smoke to prove how grownup we are. Cigarette companies understand this and aim their advertise-ment toward kids. The same is true with the pornography industry. They know that they need to hook us when we are young and keep us hooked. Pornography is a multibillion-dollar industry, but there is nothing "adult" about it. Pornography is nothing more than satisfying lustful and sinful desires. It is a demonic trick used against young kids who are just beginning to deal with the hormonal changes in their bodies. Sadly, kids are in such a hurry to grow up and become adults that they become entangled in this destructive web of sin with its resulting abortions and sexually transmitted diseases, some of which are deadly and some are incurable like herpes.

Other results of imitating the so-called adult pastimes they see glorified in "adult entertainment" are that we have a nation of unwed mothers, including many celebrated television, movie and rock stars.

Consider this: When was the last time we heard of a child who was born out of wedlock called a bastard? That shameful term, as well as its reference to sin, is no longer used in today's highly psycholo-gized society where everyone is a victim with no accountability for their actions. By the use of terms like these, societies sought to pres-sure infatuated lovers from consummating their love until they were married for the good of society and the children that resulted from their relationships. The innocent children of these couples, who could not wait until marriage, had to pay for the parents' sin by living with the stigma of that name. Even a so-called bastard child has worth in God's eyes and by His grace is able to throw off that stigma and rise above his parents' sin. For God lovingly knew that child before it was even conceived and had a plan for his or her life. Through God's sovereignty, He also provided the opportunity for that child's eternal salvation from the very foundation of the world (Romans 8:28-29)!

In today's supposedly *enlightened* society, our country has become so obsessed with sex that it becomes more difficult to discern if what we are watching on television is gratuitous sex or the selling of a product. News programs refer to "sexed-up" documents while cars and other products are referred to as "sexy." *Random House Webster's College Dictionary* defines sex appeal as "the ability to excite people sexually." Madison Avenue ad agencies are redefining the meaning and use of sex as well as our own view of what it means to be sexual beings. That is why the popular 1960s phrase, "If it *feels* good do it," became so popular. We easily recognize the sex on television ads, although knowing just exactly what the *product* is becomes a little more challenging.

Going through puberty in a sexually-charged society is not something to be envied. Again, we observe how schools may suggest that for some kids it may be alright to avoid sex, at least until they are old enough to have a meaningful relationship (whatever that means), while passing out condoms with a glance, a wink and a knowing smile. At the college level, some schools are passing out "morning after" pills to abort any conception that may have occurred the night before (ah, the benefits of a college education). Today, our kids' so-called *safe* cable channels and their worldly environments tear down generations of acceptable behavior. Passing gas and belching is portrayed as funny, and dads in most cartoon shows are portrayed as stupid. Cable outlets for kids encourage them to think, "We know our parents are *old-fashioned*, but we are smarter today than our parents were at our age. Our teachers understand and know better than our parents. Hey, even the courts are smarter and know better than our parents because *they* protect us from them. If we need to get an abortion, we can get one without our parents ever knowing about it! So I guess *that* proves how grownup we are!"

We have seen reports of some inner city males who think it is *macho* and cool to get a lot of girls pregnant. They call all of these unwed pregnancies the "jewels" in their crowns. The more jewels they have in their imaginary crowns, the greater the status. They think that the greater the status, the more manly and adult their peers will consider them to be. While the crown may be imaginary, the sad truth is that the jewels are real. They are children who will probably never know their real father once he moves on and so the cycle of poverty, hurt and depravity continues. This is not to suggest that having babies out of wedlock is considered cool only by some in the inner city. Recently on television, an entertainment segment mentioned that a female star was pregnant and the host excitedly asked the viewing audience the provocative question, "Can anyone guess who the father is?" I remember when not so long ago that having a child out of wedlock would break careers, but today it is not only approved of, but imitated as well. The Bible tells us that in the last days we would witness such things:

> Professing themselves to be wise, they became fools ….
> Wherefore God also gave them up to uncleanness through
> the lusts of their own hearts, to dishonor their own bodies
> between themselves … And even as they did not like to
> retain God in their knowledge, God gave them over to a
> reprobate mind, to do those things which are not convenient;
> being filled with all unrighteousness, fornication, wicked-
> ness, covetousness, maliciousness; full of envy, murder,
> debate, deceit, malignity; whisperers, backbiters, haters of
> God, despiteful, proud, boasters, inventors of evil things,
> disobedient to parents, Without understanding, covenant
> breakers, without natural affection, implacable, unmerciful:
> Who knowing the judgment of God, that they which commit
> such things are worthy of death, not only do the same, but
> have pleasure in them that do them …" (Romans 1:22-32).

Paul describes all of the sinful acts that we see played out everyday in our own lives and things we also find entertaining to watch. However, notice the warning we are given in verse 32: "Who knowing the judgment of God, that they which commit such things are worthy of death, not only do the same, but have pleasure in them that do them …."

Your counselee may say, "In this sexually-charged world, what is a guy going to do?" First of all, we need to look closely at "adult entertainment" and decide if it really is *adult* in nature. What is passed off as "adult" is really more in line with appealing to the pubescent curiosity of a 12-year-old child whose body is just waking up to the stirring of sexual desires. By the time we become adults, we should no longer be consumed with wondering what the opposite sex looks like naked. Instead we should have developed a moral and controlled mentality. In other words, an adult has matured to the point where they should no longer give into the whims or self-gratification without first considering the consequences of such actions. An adult is supposed to refrain from swearing or using foul language when something happens that is unpleasant or not to their liking. A tongue under control is a hallmark of a truly mature person; likewise, a body under control is characteristic of a grownup. Would you be surprised if a toddler or even a grade school kid threw a tantrum because they could not get their way? Of course not, because you know their maturity level has a long way to go before they develop self-control, yet we make excuses for bad and even sinful behavior for adults. Think about the girl being pressured to have sex with her boyfriend: "Aw, come on honey, I have my needs. If you really loved me you would have sex with me." One of the true signs of maturity is when a man becomes protective of those he loves along with being able to control his own *feelings*, urges and drives. If your counselee really loves a woman, he should not even allow himself to be in a situation with her where he can become too intimate. If your counselee does not love her, he should show her the respect God demands of us and keep his distance. If the girl is sexually loose, remind him of what the Bible says: "Do you not know that your bodies are members of Christ Himself? Shall I then take the members of Christ and unite them with a prostitute (or whore)? Never" (1 Corinthians 6:15, NIV, clarification ours)!

Speaking as one who knows, if you do not control the situation for good, the situation will control you for bad. As a former lead singer in a rock group, and long before I knew the Lord, I took advantage of many demonically setup situations, only to have regrets later. Tell your counselees that sex does not make the man, but sex can assuredly *undo* the man. The Bible clearly warns us as well as offers us hope!

> Do you not know that the wicked will not inherit the kingdom of God? Do not be deceived: Neither the sexually immoral nor idolaters nor adulterers nor male prostitutes nor homosexual offenders nor thieves nor the greedy nor drunkards nor slanderers nor swindlers will inherit the kingdom of God. And that is what some of you were. But you were washed, you were sanctified, you were justified in the name of the Lord Jesus Christ and by the Spirit of our God (1 Corinthians 6:9-11 – NIV).

Some may argue, "Well, I'm a Christian. I'm not under the Law anymore and besides, I can't help myself. I love sex. God understands. I'll still get into heaven."

If your counselee believes he is a Christian, then he will know that being sexually involved is wrong and very displeasing to God. If your counselee really loves Jesus, then he will desire to please Him more than your counselee desires to please himself. God is not a liar (Numbers 23:19). If your counselee really is in Christ, he will no longer do the things that God says will keep him out of heaven. When He tells us that the sexually immoral will not inherit the kingdom of God, He means it.

What does the Bible say about a Christian and the Law? Some Christians believe the Ten Commandments no longer apply to them. As proof that they are "saved from the Law," they are quick to point out that they go to church and perform all of the religiosity it entails. The Bible instructs us how we to test ourselves to see if we are really Christians (2 Corinthians 13:5). When we manifest the fruit of the Spirit—love, joy, peace, patience, kindness, goodness, faithfulness, gentleness and self-control, we know that we are in Christ and against these things there is no Law. However, if we continually indulge in a sinful nature, which includes sexual immorality, impurity and debauchery; idolatry and witchcraft; hatred, discord, jealousy, fits of rage, selfish ambition, dissension, ungodly favoritism, envy; drunkenness and orgies, then we have reason to be concerned (Galatians 5:16-26).

Some may argue that this seems contrary to what Paul writes earlier to the church at Corinth when he states, "All things are lawful unto me, but all things are not expedient (practical): all things are lawful for me, but I will not be brought under the power of any" (1 Corinthians 6:12, clarification ours), and again when he restates, "All things are lawful for me, but all things are not expedient (practical): all things are lawful for me, but all things edify not" (1 Corinthians 10:23, clarification ours).

If your counselees really consider themselves to be Christians but insist by saying, "God understands, I'm not under the Law anymore, I'll still get into heaven," ask them which of the Ten Commandants[1] from which they would like to be free. As a Christian, I am not under the Law either, but I can truthfully tell you that I cannot think of even *one* of the Ten Commandments that I would feel burdened to be under. Go down the list and ask, as you read the Ten Commandments, "Would you want to break this one ?" In the unlikely event that one of them should say they would like to break a certain Commandment, ask them why, and proceed from there.

The Ten Commandments

1. You shall have no other gods before Me.
2. You shall not worship any idols.
3. You shall not use God's name in vain.
4. Remember the Sabbath and keep it holy.
5. Honor your father and your mother, that your days may be long.
6. You shall not murder.
7. You shall not commit adultery.
8. You shall not steal.
9. You shall not give false testimony against your neighbor.
10. You shall not covet your neighbor's house. You shall not covet your neighbor's wife (or husband), or his manservant or maidservant, his ox or donkey, or anything that belongs to your neighbor. (Exodus 20:3-17, adapted from the NIV, clarification ours).

Paul warns us that those who are indulging themselves in sin will not inherit the kingdom of God. Paul is not being double-minded (James 1:8). He is saying that our life is to be centered in Christ and not on the world. Jesus freed Paul from being under the Law and gave him a new and godly nature. Consider for a moment the following: Can we really imagine Paul frequenting temple prostitutes and drunken orgies? That would be so out of character for Paul because his godly nature would not even consider such wickedness as an option for him. Then how are we to deal with sexual desires? Paul tells us how when he explains:

Now concerning the things whereof you wrote unto me: It is good for a man not to touch a woman. Nevertheless, to avoid fornication (sinful sex outside of marriage), let every man have his own wife, and let every woman have her own husband. Let the husband render unto the wife due benevolence: and likewise also the wife unto the husband

(1 Corinthians 7:1-3).

Even though Paul was not married at the time of his ministry, he too understood and was subjected to the same sex drive we all experience, but for him it was not troubling. In that same letter to the church at Corinth, he writes, "I say therefore to the unmarried and widows, it is good for them if they abide even as I (a virgin/restored virgin). But if they cannot contain (themselves), let them marry: for it is better to marry than to burn" (1 Corinthians 7:8-9, clarification ours). Paul understood that God created sex for the benefit of people, for their pleasure and as a means of creating a family. He also understood that God created sex with certain responsibilities and guidelines outside of which sex becomes sinful and is called fornication. We can also see this in the book of Hebrews where we read, "Marriage is honorable in all, and the bed undefiled: but whoremongers and adulterers God will judge" (Hebrews 13:4-5). Therefore, sexual expression in its proper context is not forbidden or sinful; it is only extramarital fornication that is sinful.

Jesus tells us, "If you love Me, keep My commandments" (John 14:15). When we accept Jesus as our Lord and Savior, our spirits are born-again into a new life in Christ. However, our bodies still have remnants of our old sinful nature. It is that old fleshly nature that Satan appeals to in order to lead us astray. Your counselees should be encouraged not to be discouraged. None of us are perfect. That is why we need a Savior. Because counselors and their counselees are human beings, we have to admit, "All of us have sinned and fallen short of the Glory of God" (Romans 3:23). Even Paul admitted that the godly things that he wanted to do he failed to do, and the sinful thing he was trying to avoid doing, was the very thing he actually ended up doing (Romans 7:15)! Sometimes your counselees do not start out to sin, but something happens. They may get angry and say things they should not have said, or they react in an ungodly manner to a situation. Perhaps a picture at the magazine stand catches their eye and instead of dismissing it and looking away, they allow themselves another peek and dwell upon the picture that will release sinful desires. If counselees *truly* regret having done those things and ask God for the strength to resist the temptation the next time it comes against them, then God knows that they have acknowledged their struggle to change and He will help them to resist. In other words, if we submit ourselves to God and resist the devil, he will flee from us (James 4:7). None of us can indulge ourselves in doing what we know is wrong and excuse our actions by reasoning, "It's okay, I'm not under the Law anymore and besides, no one was hurt. I know God loves me anyway. He understands my needs and won't hold it against me. After all, I *am* a Christian. I go to church and even teach Sunday school. Heck, I'll just do it and ask for forgiveness later!" If this is this how your counselees really think, then we must be very concerned that possibly your counselees are not saved because they are more interested in pleasing themselves than they are in pleasing God. Remember, they may be able to fool us or themselves, but they cannot fool God (Galatians 6:7)! If Christ is in your counselees, not only do they have the hope for deliverance from sexual tempta- tion, there is no doubt that they *will* also be able to reach the goal of living the life of godly virgin men. It would be good, however, to reinforce your counselees with the concept that being tempted is not a sin; giving into the temptation (by uncontrolled thoughts, words or deeds) is what is sinful.

It may be good to pause here and reflect upon words of hope that Jesus gives us when He says, referring to Himself, "For God sent not His Son into the world to condemn the world; but that the world through Him might be saved" (John 3:17) because, "The Lord is not slack (uncaring) concerning His promise, as some men count slackness (uncaring); but is longsuffering toward us, not willing that any should perish, but that all should come to repentance" (2 Peter 3:9, clarification ours). God is not looking for loopholes in order to deny us eternal salvation and to punish us for our sinful deeds, but rather He offers us a simple and basic way for us to be saved. If we accept Jesus as our Lord and Savior and, "If we confess our sins, He is faithful and just to forgive us our sins, and to cleanse us from all unrighteousness" (1 John 1:9). However, just because Jesus understands how susceptible we are to sin, and because He knows that we struggle against our fallen nature and wants to help us change, your counselees must not be lulled into a false sense of security that Jesus is being permissive toward those sins he keeps struggling against. Paul warns us, "What shall we say then? Shall we continue in sin, that grace may abound? God forbid" (Romans 6:1-2a). Sanctification is an ongoing struggle for as long as we live, but through Jesus we are able to overcome those challenges we face as we grow in Christ. Nevertheless, as the Apostle Peter warns us, "If they have escaped the corruption of the world by knowing our Lord and Savior Jesus Christ and are again entangled in it and overcome (by it), they are worse off at the end than they were at the beginning" (2 Peter 2:20, NIV, clarification ours). While God offers us salvation through Christ and understands that from time to time we will backslide into sinful situations, we must not take God's love and salvation through Christ for granted and figure it is alright if we give into our lust once in awhile. Each time we give into sin, it becomes more difficult to overcome the next time we are tempted. Remember, it is common knowledge that the more time we can put between us and a specific sin or a bad habit, the easier it is to resist that sin or bad habit.

Your counselee may ask, "I really want to stop sinning, but are you saying if I keep backsliding that I am going to hell even though I accepted Christ as my Savior?" As a Christian counselor, we know God understands that everyone struggles against all sorts of temptations. Jesus understands this when He counsels, "Watch and pray, that you enter not into temptation: the spirit indeed is willing, but the flesh is weak" (Matthew 26:41; Mark 14: 38). If your counselee really loves God, but still finds himself in sin and feels shame and guilt, he is confirming that he is a Christian even though he is struggling one. Your Counselee must realize that they should not allow themselves to continue in the cycle of *sin, guilt, confession, sin* because they are not struggling against the sin that they love, but rather they are settling into a cycle that is acceptable to them and, therefore, becomes a sinful routine.

Paul writes, "Wherefore, my beloved, as you have always obeyed, not as in my presence only, but now much more in my absence, work out your own salvation with fear and trembling" (Philippians 2:12).

In the beginning of this passage, Paul is saying that our struggle to grow in our salvation is real only if we continue to work at it when no one is around to pressure us not to sin. Your counselee may argue, "I thought we were saved by grace and not by works?" We are saved by grace, which is an undeserved gift from God (Ephesians 2:8-9). They may understand it better this way.

This about this: If several children each receive a plot of land for a strawberry patch completely seeded and supplied with a hose for watering the garden, it becomes the property of the child. It is now up to the child to take care of his new gift. If he waters it and pulls the weeds, he is assured of a wonderful garden with lots of fruit. On the other hand, if the child begins tending his garden with great enthusiasm, but starts getting lazy and only waters the garden occasionally and pulls out some of the weeds leaving other weeds to grow, he will still have some fruit; however, not as much or as healthy because he allowed the weeds to rob the fruit of its space to grow and its source of nourishment. Finally, if the child enthusiastically begins working in his garden, but soon gets distracted with other projects, some strawberries will still grow, but he will have very few unhealthy strawberries because the fruits struggle to compete with all of the weeds. As a result, this child will produce some fruit, but not as much as the child who is really committed to working in his garden. All of the children have gardens, but it is easy to see the amount of commitment each child puts into his garden by observing the healthy fruit. The same is true with our salvation. God offers us the gift of salvation through the payment Jesus made for us through His sacrifice on the Cross. Once your counselee receives salvation, he needs to work on perfecting it so that it is reflected by his actions; which is accomplished by eliminating the weeds of sin in his life in order to allow good spiritual fruit to be produced.

If we are no longer under the Law, how are we to we deal with the Ten Commandments? The Ten Commandments are God's guideposts intended to make our journey safer through life. Consider this: Think about when you learned to drive. At first you memorized the driver's manual with all its laws and warnings. Then you passed the driving and written tests; after awhile you were no longer concerned with referencing the driver's manual or, for instance, what to do when approaching an intersection. Now you drive with the confidence of a seasoned driver who instinctively knows what to do. The law has now become an internalized habit of your driving skills and you no longer need to think or *worry* about it. This is how it is with God's Law. Occasionally, we see "crazy" drivers doing rolling stops or running red lights and passing on the shoulder of the road. While you would never intentionally run a red light or drive in such a foolish manner, the other driver is driving under the law because laws are made for careless people like him. If we are in Christ and He in us, we no longer need the law to check our rebellious and evil hearts because we are now new law-abiding creatures in Him, not out of fear of the law, but because we now obey the law instinctively. Even if you had run a red light and did not get caught, you would still feel badly about it!

Nevertheless, counselees must be careful. Even when they internalize God's Word and have overcome their sinful desires, they can become blindsided by Satan as I have discovered for myself. On one occasion, I had a sin that I struggled against and just when it seemed I had mastered it, that sin would pop up some place unexpectedly; even though I knew I should not look or think about it, I paused just for a moment. That was long enough for that sin's hook to snag me! Before I knew it, I was thinking, "Maybe if I just skirt around the perimeter it will be okay; after all, no one is being hurt." The next thing I knew, that old sin I thought I was rid of came back at me with a vengeance! I had to start dealing all over again with ridding myself of an infectious and habit-forming sin. Therefore, I would admonish your counselees, "Why would you even want to flirt with that old sin and the demons behind it?" Jesus not only understands the dangers of *revisiting* an old sin from "a safe distance," but He also understands what is behind it and what we are really up against. He warns us:

When an evil spirit comes out of a man (freeing you from your sin), it goes through arid places seeking rest and does not find it. Then it says, 'I will return to the house I left' (which is your heart and mind). When it arrives, it finds the house unoccupied, swept clean and put in order. Then it goes and takes with it seven other spirits more wicked than itself (to help it seduce you back into your old sinful habits), and they go in and live there. And the final condition of that man is worse than the first. That is how it will be with this wicked generation (Matthew 12:43-45, NIV, clarification ours).

When your counselees "accidentally" come across an old sin that they think they will be safe from if they only entertain it from a "safe distance," they should be made fully aware that it is a demonic trap specifically set for them, and it is seven times more potent than they could ever imagine! Your counselee should be encouraged not to give up, but be aware that there are no such things as accidents or luck, and realize that whatever temptations may come their way they will be able, through Christ, to resist and overcome them. The first thing your counselees must do when they face temptation is quickly submit themselves to God. Resist the devil and he will flee (Philippians 4:13; James 4:7). If your counselee does this, Satan will see God standing by their side with His great arm around your counselees' shoulders and staring right back at them! As your counselees struggle against their flesh, and are really sincere about changing their lifestyle into a life that is pleasing to God, *they will* overcome. God looks at the true desires of our hearts and while He also knows our weaknesses, He does not allow them to be used as an excuse for us to return to those old sinful habits.

The next term we need to deal with is macho or manly. We live in a world that glamorizes sex, violence and rock-'n-roll. Sex is wonderful, but so is junk food; if that is all we indulge in, we are in for a lot of trouble. To begin with, the reason sex is so wonderful is because God made it to be wonderful, but sex is also addicting. Like drugs, if it is used for the purpose it was intended for, our lives and well-being are assured. However, if mistreated, what was meant for good can become deadly — literally!

In the previous chapter we compared the anticipation of someone's wedding night to the opening of birthday gifts. To expand on this a little more, have your counselee think back to when he was a child before Christmas day. If he came upon some unwrapped presents that were meant for him and he yielded to the temptation to explore and maybe even play with the toys a little, which presents attracted him the most when Christmas morning came? Was it the wrapped ones he recognized by their shape or the mysterious large package lying under the tree that he did not recognize? Which one would your counselee want to open first? Would it be the package he already knew about or the new and exciting wrapped one? What if one of the presents he recognized as a toy a friend of his received as a birthday present, but got tired of and rewrapped it as a Christmas gift for him? Would it mean more if it was unopened and still in the bubble pack? Sex is the same way. The wonderful present your counselee would wish to give and receive is the one no one has seen or played with. Preserving *your counselee's* virginity is just as an important gift for his future wife to receive as it is for him. Tell him to not exchange those gifts *before* he is married.

I have two friends who are both professing Christians. One is a mega recording star; the other one was a backup singer with his group. When our group of entertainers met at a friend's home for fellowship, the recording artist was there and confessed his deep love for a woman and asked if it was wrong to engage in sex with her. We discussed what the Bible had to say about sex before marriage, but my friend was not totally convinced. He reasoned, like so many others I have counseled, that God created sex and He knew how much they *really* loved each other. He questioned how it could feel so right it if it was wrong; they were eventually going to get married anyway, so he was positive God would not disapprove. I really believe he loved her and there was no doubt in my mind that she was totally devoted to and in love with him, but while they consummated their relationship, they never got married and they are living separate lives today.

Sex can be deceiving if we let it. Make no mistake—we live in a world that says sex with anyone at anytime is acceptable as long as both parties agree but to do so, knowing that God calls sex without marriage a sin, is to put your counselees in a dangerous position. The world says that Christians do not want your counselees to have any fun, but that is a lie from the pit of Hell. God *does* want your counselees to have fun and that includes sexual pleasure too, but only in the way He intended, in a marriage between a man and a woman.

Who better understands the inner workings of an automobile and is better able to tell you how to take care and maintain it for the maximum pleasure and enjoyment—the inventor of the car or someone who only knows how to put in gas and drive the car? We do not all maintain our cars according to the manufacturer's guidelines. I am guilty too, but if we neglect our cars, it is only a matter of time before we have to replace a transmission or engine because we do not follow the manufacturer's instructions and believe me, it is an expensive mistake. Like the auto, we need to maintain ourselves according to the manufacturer's maintenance manual (the Bible).

Men take a lot of pride in their cars. Many of us wash and wax that baby all the time. We invest in expensive sound systems, tricked-out bodies and interiors with extravagant chrome wheels. We do not even like someone to look at our car's paint job Cross-eyed because they might scratch it! Male counselees need to treat the women in their lives better than they treat their cars. They need to respect women and be protective of them. In doing so, they will become more adult and more of a man.

To those of your counselees who have kept their virginity, they need to be assured that that they are in good company. Consider for a moment the One through whom all things were made and who is able, with just a passing thought, think something into or out of existence (John 1:1-3). Why would such a One care about your counselee? Why would such a One humiliate Himself by putting on the body of a mere man and subject Himself to all kinds of temptations, including those of a sexual nature? If men, as mere humans, know how hard it is to struggle against sexual temptation and know how much guys *really* want to give into those urges, your counselee may wonder, "Why would *anyone*, especially God, want to come to earth and subject Himself to being imprisoned in a male body with all of those raging hormones?" That is exactly what Jesus did for our sake. The Bible says, "For we do not have a high priest who is unable to sympathize with our weaknesses, but we have one who has been tempted in every way, just as we are—yet was without sin" (Hebrews 4:15, NIV). Wow! What a man! He was tempted in all ways just like we are, including dealing with raging hormones as a lad, yet He remained a virgin. Jesus was no wimp—the Bible says He was a carpenter. Carpenters in Israel not only worked with wood but with stone as well. I have been to Israel and can tell you that it would be difficult to find any wooden houses—everything is made of stone. The point is that to have been a carpenter in Israel required a man of great strength and stamina. There were no sissies on those jobs. Jesus was every bit a man as any man I know, but He had strength under control.

When your counselee is with his date, does he try to force himself on her, or is he a man who exhibits his strength under control? A real man does not have to force his will on anyone, but rather submits his will to the One who made him and loves him the most. Today, we find it difficult to hear, much less accept, the words sin, shame, submit and the phrase, "boundaries of right and wrong." We have become so psychologized that we are told, and unfortunately believe, that we are not at fault, but that we are really victims of situations or the actions of others. Not only do many of us not understand what it means to sin, we cannot even contemplate the concept, and that is to our disadvantage.

Because men are visual creatures, we are stimulated by what we see or things we visualize. Everywhere we look sex is bombarding us. Even when we do not have sex on our minds, something flashes before us and *feelings* and emotions begin to stir. Think about how you could innocently be searching the web and all of a sudden there it is, PORN. Or maybe you open an e-mail and jumping right out of your computer is PORN! Soft, as well as hard core, pornography can be seen in television shows, news programs, "R" and even some "PG" rated movies. As we previously observed, sex has become so much a part of our thoughts that now inanimate objects are called sexy and news reports of official government documents are described by the media as being "sexed-up." Even the despicable profession of being a "pimp," which is the lowest form of a man who sells women's bodies for sex, is used as a cool term. Music and rap spit out filth and obscenities as well as degrading women and sex. Men and women alike use the "F" word in everyday casual conversations. As we discussed at the beginning of the chapter, even television commercials are selling you herbal preparations and drugs to help you get turned on. It has been said that as the more perverse things become *normalized*, we will soon reach the saturation point where there is nothing left to *normalize*. Anything and *everything* will become acceptable. How can a man deal with this?

First of all, counselees must accept responsibility for their own actions as well as any consequences of those actions. They must do the best they can to eliminate the triggers that set off their hormones and sinful urges. Counselees must admit that they are sinners because if they do not, then they are unable to fight against the sin that is in them, and the sinful world that is trying to seduce them. Counselees must know their enemy before they can defeat him. Then they must put Scripture into their thought lives. Counselees must also make use of Scripture by putting verses from the Bible in accessible places where the Scriptures will do them the most good by constantly reminding them of how God wants them to live. One example would be, in dealing with pornography, to type or write out a couple of verses from Psalm 101:

> **I will behave myself wisely** in a perfect way. O when wilt Thou come unto me? **I will walk within my house with a perfect heart. <u>I will set no wicked thing before mine eyes</u>:** I hate the work of them that turn aside; it shall not cleave to (get a hold of) me (Psalm 101:2-3, emphasis and clarification ours).

Little reminders like these Scriptures, along with memorizing them, will help counselees; but they must truly believe God's Word and apply them to their lives. If something pornographic comes on television, they must switch it off and reread the above passage of Scripture. Better yet, they would be well advised to turn the off television altogether. Another good Scripture to learn and draw upon when temptation comes knocking, is a passage from a Psalm that David composed as a prayer of repentance after he too fell into sexual sin:

Create in me a clean heart, O God; and renew a right spirit within me. Cast me not away from Your presence; and take not Your Holy Spirit from me. Restore unto me the joy of Your salvation; and uphold me with Your free Spirit (Psalm 51:10-13).

Encourage counselees not to give up. Men can maintain their virginity and if they have already lost it, they can and must restore it. The battleground is in our hearts and minds, and the way to overcome and win that battle is with the Bible. By counselees having a Scriptural game plan, with God's help, the victory is theirs.

We begin our battle with Scripture because it is God's Word and, therefore, can be trusted to set us free from all of our sins. Jesus says, "… I am the way, the truth, and the life: no man comes unto the Father, but by Me" (John 14:6). This is important because the Bible tells us that Jesus is the Word of God (John 1:1-3); therefore, because Jesus is the Word of God and the Truth of God, we may feel confident when we believe in Him and put biblical principles into practice. "And you shall know the truth, and the truth shall make you free" (John 8:32). Perhaps your counselee may say, "You don't know my problem with sex. I am really addicted and I can't stop. My counselor tells me I am a sex addict and I will always be in recovery. There are some things I can't even tell my psychologist because I'm so bad."

It is important for counselees to realize that whenever people seek help through secular psychology (psychiatry), they are doomed to always be in "recovery," with no hope of ever being truly free of their "disease." The Bible addresses the philosophy of secular psychology and other Gnostic philosophies of men when it warns us, "Beware least any man spoil you through philosophy and vain deceit, after the tradition of men, after the rudiments of the world, and not after Christ" (Colossians 2:8), and Christ *is* the truth (John 14:6a). Most beliefs of men are in direct opposition to what God promises, which is, you can be delivered from sin.

The Bible teaches, and this is fundamental for your counselee's recovery, that when they accept Jesus as their Lord, they can be delivered from sexual sin. Jesus says, "… whosoever commits

155

sin is the servant of sin" (John 8:34), but He goes on to promise us, "If the Son therefore shall make you free, you shall be free indeed" (John 8:36). Your counselee may still insist, "You don't know my thought life. I really have *sick* fantasies." That kind of thinking is just one more of Satan's lies. Again your counselee is not *sick*; that is just more psychobabble. Sickness is brought on by a physical pathogen that infects the body and causes physical ailments. "If you are sick," secular psychologists argue, "then your problem is not your fault. After all, who could be mad at someone who caught a cold, for instance?" Your counselee's thoughts are sinful temptations (not an illness), and being tempted is not a sin; giving into the temptation is the sin. Educate your counselees not to be discouraged about those evil and perverted thoughts. They can overcome them. They are not the only ones who have had such sinful thoughts. The Bible encourages us, "There hath no temptation taken you but such as is common to man: but God is faithful, who will not suffer (allow) you to be tempted above that (which) you are able; but will with the temptation also make a way to escape, that you may be able to bear it" (1 Corinthians 10:13, clarification ours). God understands their struggle with sex. He created it. As your counselees mature, they have to fill their minds with good things to replace the wicked things on which they allow their minds to dwell.

The Apostle, toward the conclusion of his letter to the church at Philippi writes, "Finally, brethren, whatsoever things are true, whatsoever things are honest, whatsoever things are just, whatsoever things are pure, whatsoever things are lovely, whatsoever things are of good report; if there be any virtue, and if there be any praise, think on these things" (Philippians 4:8). Our thought lives open the door to our active lives. Fantasies, after they have been nurtured and constantly thought about, give birth to real life actions; therefore, we must stop those thoughts before they take root. If they have already taken root, then we must crowd them out by dwelling upon edifying thoughts, which is what Paul was encouraging us to do in this passage.

Your counselee may ask, "Can God, right this moment, deliver me totally from evil thoughts, help me not to look at pornography and enable me to stop having sinful desires and masturbating?" As a biblical counselor, you are able to answer with confidence, "Of course He can." Mary, the mother of Jesus, confirms, "For with God nothing shall be impossible" (Luke 1:37), and Jesus Himself says as much in Matthew 19:26 and Mark 10:27. However, not every blind person who Jesus healed showed evidence of being healed right away. With some, He interacted by making clay out of His saliva and dirt and told the blind person to go and wash his eyes, thereby forcing the man to participate in his healing (John 9:6-7). With another, He moistened the blind man's eyes with His saliva and then laid hands on him but when the man opened his eyes, he was only partially delivered from his blindness; Jesus laid His hands on the blind man a second time, and this time the man's sight was completely restored (Mark 8:22-26). Presumably the man needed to strengthen his faith and not give up his belief that Jesus could heal him. Although God is able to heal us right away, He does not always do so. For whatever reason, God allows us to struggle with our deliverance. We must not give up or be discouraged if we backslide.

Just like the psychiatrists, Satan will tell your counselees (men and women) that they cannot do it or that if they stop indulging themselves in their lustful ways, it is only temporary and that they will fail and repeat their sin again. What does God have to say about that? God knows the limits of mankind. He also knows we can be freed from sin. Like the blind man Jesus had to lay His hands on twice, God knows your counselee can be completely delivered from his sexual sins. God gives us encouragement when He says, "For a just man falls seven times, and rises up again: but the wicked shall fall into mischief" (Proverbs 24:16). God knows we are going to struggle until we get it right, but it is the wicked or unsaved man who, when he falls into mischief (sin), likes it and stays there! Men who go to the gym to build those macho muscles begin with weights they can handle. As they become stronger, they increase the weights and develop their bodies into beautifully sculptured works of physical art. So it is with faith and sin. As we continue to strengthen our faith and commit ourselves to rejecting lust, we eventually overcome our sin and restore our masculine virginity, thereby becoming virtuous men.

Jesus promises, "If the Son therefore shall make you free, you shall be free indeed" (John 8:36). Remember what the Apostle Paul writes, "I can do all things through Christ which strengthens me" (Philippians 4:13). Some people believe that Paul may have been a widower; we do know that Paul lived a chaste (virgin) life. He was every bit a man in his life, being beaten and jailed for the sake of the gospel. Paul was so committed to the Gospel of Jesus Christ that he gave his life for it. It takes a real man to stand up and take the abuse unto death for that in which he believes. During the first-century, many Christians were being persecuted and many of the men were tortured and killed. In that Middle Eastern society, women were dependent on the males in their family for protection and support. That is why a girl stayed with her father until she was married. Having sons was important too because if a husband died, there would be a male heir to protect and defend the poor widow. Because of the wholesale persecution and killing of Christians, Paul believed that if there was no stirring of sexual urges within the woman, they should remain unmarried, at least until the political situation would hopefully change; and then they would be safe to marry without the threat of officials or Roman soldiers invading their homes and taking away their husbands. Paul also offered the same advice to the young men. If they could keep their sexual urges under control, it would be better for them not to marry because it would put their wives in jeopardy of becoming widows.

One of the best ways to avoid awakening sexual urges is to keep from being too close or touching each other. Above all, do not allow yourself any sexual intercourse or fornication as the Bible calls it. Paul knew that men could control the natural desire to have sex because he was able to refrain from fornication and held up his virginity as an example to follow. Paul also understood that not everyone was as able to resist sexual sin, so he advised those who were struggling to go ahead and get married rather than commit a sin against their beloved, themselves and even more importantly, against God (1 Corinthians 7:1-9).

Earlier in this chapter we used a Scripture from one of Paul's letters of inspired instruction to the church at Corinth that not only offers good advice, but also basic common sense that will help all of us escape sexual temptations. It reads, "Be ye not unequally yoked together with unbelievers: for what fellowship hath righteousness with unrighteousness? and what communion has light with darkness" (2 Corinthians 6:14)? Paul is telling us that we should break away from those relationships and places we have been hanging around that encourages us to joke, look and even sexually act out because it only serves to arouse our sexual desires directly or indirectly. We need to find godly new friends and places to hang around that will give us accountability and support. "Maybe I can help my friends become Christians if I still see them," or "If I keep dating her, maybe she'll change!" We tell people who we counsel, "No missionary dating."

There is an old saying, "One bad apple spoils the whole barrel." A long time ago many products were shipped in barrels. Every town had their own barrel makers who were known as coopers. That is where the family name Cooper originated. The grocer would open up all of the barrels which contained all kinds of various items from nails to crackers, pickles and fruits and line them up to display their contents for sale. However, there was no air conditioning and because everything in a barrel was packed fairly tight, the grocer wanted to make sure that no spoiled produce would be allowed in the barrel with the good produce because he knew, as in the case of our apple, as the fruit spoiled it would "infect" the apples around it, which in turn would infect the apples around them; soon the whole barrel would be filled with spoiled and rotting apples. Once that happened, all of the produce would have to be thrown out at a great financial loss to the grocer. If this was allowed to happen too many times, the poor man would be broke and his family would suffer. Do you think that if you had a barrel of spoiled apples and you put the one good apple in the barrel with all of the spoiled apples, the goodness would rub off on the bad apples causing the bad apples to miraculously become good once more? Of course not. The same applies with your counselee. Your counselee cannot hang around with people who will keep exposing him to sexually stimulating conversations, entertainment and actual encounters.

Remember in the last chapter the Bible story about our virgin hero named Joseph? The man he was working for had a wife who wanted to have a little sex with a cute Hebrew hunk while her husband was away, but when she tried to seduce him, Joseph said, "... how then can I do this great wickedness, and sin against God" (Genesis 39:9)? However, as you remember, this was a very determined woman. She grabbed Joseph by his clothes and told him to lie with her but Joseph turned and as the Bible states, he "fled" (verse 11).

This is exactly what your counselee should do when placed in that type of situation, be it real or imagined (i.e., movies or pornographic material). Plainly stated, your counselee must dump his old friends who will drag him into sin, and get away from those sexy girls who dress with everything showing and only want your counselee for his physical body. He must flee from this temptation!!!! This type of commitment shows that your counselee is taking responsibility for his own actions. Your counselee should surround himself with godly friends whose relationships will edify God and him.

Remaining a virgin is not for sissies. It takes a *real* man, a *strong* man to keep himself a virgin until he finds that special someone he has been waiting and keeping himself for until his wedding night. It is still possible to find good role models living in the world of the twenty-first century. Earlier we discussed some movers and shakers in the entertainment business who restored their virginity and remained chaste until they got married. This is a great accomplishment; most of us are never tempted to the extent entertainers are. Women are constantly throwing themselves at them; it is not uncommon for entertainers to receive pictures of women in suggestive poses who hope the entertainer will pay some attention to them.

Just a short time before this writing, there was a popular ABC television network reality show entitled, "The Bachelor." The show consisted of twenty-five beautiful women trying to get the very handsome bachelor to ask one of them to marry him. The intrigue of the show was its appeal to the audience's suppressed voyeurism. (Voyeurism is a third party enjoying sex by fantasizing that he or she is involved in sexual relations through the people they are secretly watching.) The participants of the show conducted themselves in varying degrees of sexual behavior and the viewer, like the decadent Romans of old, watched the debauchery (immoral activity) with eyes that hungered for more. The whole world watched as the people involved in the show became rich and famous overnight.

There was a handsome and successful young man by the name of Jason Illian watching the show who was dismayed at what he was seeing. Jason was a virgin, but he was not a loser as many guys might think about a guy who was almost 30 and never had sex. Jason is not only a very handsome and single young man; he graduated Magna Cum Laude from Texas Christian University with a B.S. in International Finance. Not only was Jason a finalist for a Rhodes scholarship, he was also vice president of a multibillion-dollar international company.

Around the same time, ABC had a new idea for another reality series called "The Bachelorette." In this show, the "game" is a reversal of "The Bachelor" where twenty-five handsome young men live together in a mansion and try to get a beautiful bachelorette to choose one of them as a husband.

In a television interview, Jason told how he went from watching "The Bachelor" with dismay to becoming a finalist in "The Bachelorette" when a friend, who Jason was discussing his dismay over the morals he had witnessed on "The Bachelor," suggested Jason try to get an audition for the show. He thought that perhaps Jason could bring a different perspective to the show and thus, make a statement for morality. Jason contacted ABC, and a few months later he was called for an audition. However, during the interview Jason confessed to the producers, "I'm not sure this will be a good fit for who I am." To Jason's surprise, "The next thing I know I am getting off a plane in New York saying, 'What have I gotten myself into now?' "

The show was a big hit and no doubt many girls developed a crush on him. As the show progressed, the number of rivals Jason had to compete with kept getting smaller and smaller. Twenty-five became twenty. Twenty became fifteen and then finally fourteen. To Jason, each passing week must have seemed like hearing your neighbor above you taking off his shoes before going to bed. You hear the first shoe drop, but as the time keeps passing, you keep listening and waiting for the other shoe to drop. Half of the competition was over and now it was Jason's time to be rejected. He reflects on that moment in the show when it became his turn to leave. "My belief system for the most part seemed so foreign to them," Jason reflects. "I knew I wasn't a good fit for Jen," referring to the bachelorette on the show. Jason recalls the reason he first agreed to do the show. "I went on the program to *show love* rather than to find it." He continues:

> The sword of the Spirit (is an) offensive weapon in Ephesians 6. It simply says it is a sword but it is a double-edged sword and one blade is your faithfulness to what you believe (be)cause our faithfulness to the Lord, that's our power but the other side of it is relevance. It's the relevance to our culture. It's a double edged-sword. You've got to be able to swing it both ways ... everybody says, 'Well you speak on abstinence.' No, I really speak on sex because sex is something God created and it's a wonderful thing, but it's a wonderful thing when it's kept in the right context and ... it's kind of like fire. Fire's great if it warms our food, it heats our houses but you take that same fire out and you put it in the middle of the living room, it just burns your house to the ground. I want to become the right person and I know that will attract the right people to me. The biggest misconception is that you have to be sleeping around ... that's the cool thing to do and you're not really a man otherwise .... I'm not out there to change everybody's viewpoint on things. I'm just here to live my life and especially talk to the men and say, 'Listen if you really want to be a leader, if you really want to have an impact and leave a legacy, it is more than just sleeping around. It is understanding who you are and becoming that type of leader so the women in our lives feel like ... they're being served and that they're special and that they have a place in our heart(s) and when you change the men, then you also change the women.[1]

Since most men like sports, let me conclude by sharing an interview I recently saw given by Andy Pettitte. As most of you guys know, Andy is one of the all time great pitchers in major league baseball. He began his career as a pitcher for the New York Yankees and has a post-season record of 13 winning games, a winning streak that began with his professional debut on May 27, 1995, and ran for 10 seasons straight. The only major league pitcher in the history of baseball to do better than Andy is another Yankee pitcher, Babe Ruth! Andy led his team to six American League pennants and won four World Series!!! What really sets Andy apart as a real major league champion and role model is that Andy Pettitte was a virgin when he got married. With his shy and unassuming boy next-door grin, Andy looked right into the camera and unashamedly stated, "Me and my wife did not have sex until we were married. It became something that was very important to both of us that we were committed to each other waiting until we were married." In talking about his dependency on Jesus on the mound, Andy made a statement that can be easily applied to his commitment to remaining a virgin until marriage, "I just think it relates to your Christian faith. If you do the work, if you're in the Bible like you need to be, if you're praying to the Lord, you're gonna stay in the game a lot longer, and you're gonna be a lot stronger than other people that aren't."

Promiscuous sexual relationships have been celebrated in song and on the screen. They promote that love is a game people play. However, if you want to stop playing games and you have a desire to keep your romance special and avoid sexual sin, take Andy's advice. "... if you're in the Bible like you need to be, if you're praying to the Lord, you're gonna stay in the game a lot longer, and you're gonna be a lot stronger than other people that aren't."[2] This advice comes directly from the mouth of a *real* man. Andy agrees that you need to stay in the Bible. When you seek advice from God and apply it to your life, you will not regret it. While the whole world around you is going crazy trying to fulfill their sexual lusts, you can stay strong, "... because greater is He (Jesus) that is in you, than he (Satan) that is in the world" (1 John 4:4b, clarification ours). So, like Andy Pettitte, take your Bible and read it, believe it, stand on it and apply it to your life. Become a real man, and stand your ground as a virgin for Christ.

"Yes," your counselee may say, "but those guys probably never allowed themselves to become sexually active. Once you start having sex it's not that easy to stop." Your counselee may possibly challenge you with, "Can you give an example of a sexually active man who stopped and was able to restore his virginity?" That is a good point. The truth is that once a person starts allowing their body to satisfy its sexual pleasures, you are correct—it is not all that easy to stop. It is like any sin; the first time a person knowingly sins, their conscience troubles them, but the more often they give into sinful desires, the easier it is to continue doing it until their conscience becomes so singed that sinning becomes second nature. They may never give another thought to the fact that they are now immersed in sin. As with the example Dr. Frank Wilson gave us earlier, they let out the beast in the basement.

A story comes to mind regarding a church supervisor who had to deal with such a problem. The church was located in a liberal college town that opened its doors to anyone who wanted to join. Like most college towns, this town was very *modern* in their thinking so this church tried not to be "judgmental" in its approach to the gospel. Because of the activities of some of its members (one member was having sex with his stepmother), you could conclude that the concept of sin was never addressed because the church leadership did not want anyone to feel uncomfortable. What a *progressive* college town church! Think about this for a moment: The man having sex with his stepmother not only lost his virginity before he was married, but because he was having sex with his stepmother, he was not only a *fornicator*, but an *adulterer* who was committing *incest* as well! Talk about "three strikes and you're out." This guy was on the fast track to Hell.

Sadly, you are probably not particularly shocked to find this kind of scenario being played out in your own *enlightened college* or *sophisticated town*. After all, it is not *politically correct* to judge other people's lifestyles, and many seeker-friendly churches only want to focus on positive messages. However, the truth is that this was not a modern church, but the first-century church at Corinth, and the church supervisor was the Apostle Paul. Solomon says, "... there is no new thing under the sun" (Ecclesiastes 1:9). So how did Paul handle this problem? He wrote to the church at Corinth and advised them that this kind of conduct was not at all acceptable, and that they had to confront the young man and tell him to stop his sinful action:

> It is actually reported that there is sexual immorality among you, and of a kind that does not occur even among pagans: A man has his father's wife. And you are proud! Shouldn't you rather have been filled with grief and have put out of your fellowship the man who did this? (1 Corinthians 5:1-2, NIV).

Paul is saying that the church at Corinth not only knew about this disgraceful act, they tolerated it—not unlike some liberal churches we find today: "... not only do the same, but have pleasure in them that do them" (Romans 1:32b). This young man must have thought he was really something—Mr. Macho himself! Nevertheless, he was simply reflecting the fast-paced society in which he lived. "Yeah," your counselee may argue, "but he didn't live in the kind of world we live in today. We have to deal with TV and all kinds of sexual assaults. Back then they did not have the same pressures. It was a much different and low tech world compared to today!" You are correct, but listen to what they had to deal with. To begin with, Corinth, like Berkley was a college town that not only allowed experimentation but encouraged it as well. Corinth was also a pagan city that had 12 pagan temples, the largest of which was dedicated to Aphrodite, the goddess of love. The word *aphrodisiac* (anything you consume that heightens sexual arousal) has its root in the name Aphrodite. The temple of Aphrodite encouraged fornication by having sexual rituals for devotees to engage in with its many temple prostitutes. In the center of Corinth was the ancient temple of Apollo, the male Greek god of love. This certainly was a very sensuous, free-spirited and materialistic place to live in, probably not so very different than where you or I live, but in spite of all of Corinth's promiscuity and materialism, it was the very best place for the body of Christ to be as long as the church impacted the community rather than the community impacting the church as we observe in many of our seeker-friendly churches. It is no wonder that the church at Corinth was a little indulgent toward this young man; after all, no one would want to be accused of not being broad-minded or intolerant in this so-called *enlightened* community.

Paul was not concerned about what other people thought; he was more concerned with the souls of those who professed their faith in Christ that they would not fall back into sin and become a snare to the others, as well as reflecting badly on Christ. So Paul warned the church that if the young man would not repent, it would be better to put him out of the body of Christ rather than to allow him to stay and contaminate others. If he would not repent and stop his abominable lifestyle, then he could go to the devil, and hopefully that would help him realize that his actions were destructive to his soul. If he repented and restored his virginity (cease his fornication until marriage), he could return to the body of Christ. The young man would not repent, so the church at Corinth told him to leave (giving him over to the devil), trusting that he would see the error of his ways, that his spirit might eventually be saved (1 Corinthians 5:5). The good news is that in Paul's second letter to the church at Corinth, we read that the young man eventually did repent and was once again restored to the body of Christ. Nevertheless, some of the Corinthians were finding it hard to forgive and forget, so Paul admonished them by saying that it was their duty to welcome him back with love to prevent bringing sin upon themselves by driving this repentant young man back into the arms of the world and causing him to fall again (2 Corinthians 2:1-11). Since we do not read of further sexual problems with him, we may conclude that he too restored his virginity and became a new creature in Christ (2 Corinthians 5:17)! Paul knew that with God's help we can be free from the sin of sexual immorality and be restored once again as a virgin man of God; when the Son sets you free, you are free indeed (John 8:36). Jesus says it, I read it, I believe it, and I receive it. The good news for your counselee is that he can be set free too!

A Practical Application for the Male Virgin

Create in me a clean heart, O God;
and renew a right (virgin) spirit within me.

Cast me not away from Your presence;
and take not Your Holy Spirit from me.

Restore unto me the joy of Your salvation;
and uphold me with Your free Spirit.

(Psalm 51:10-12, clarification ours)

As Christian counselors, we should all know the memorization and application of Scripture in our counselee's heart is vital if they are to ever be freed from the bondage of sexual lusts. While it is helpful and encouraging for men to place Scriptures around the areas where temptations have a way of attacking us (dashboard of the car, the telephone, on our computers at home and at work, next to the television screen, etc.), we must also memorize Scriptures and even include them in our prayers. We must pray at least once everyday, preferably more. How do you encourage your counselees to do that? Have them think about the times their mind starts to drift or they "mull" something over in their minds during the day. That is the perfect time to bring God into their thought life. Prayers are the way we communicate with God. They do not have to be formal. We can include God in our thoughts when we think (talk) to ourselves. If your counselees spend a lot of time in their car, that is a great time to pray. Jesus promises in John 8:36, "Whom the Son sets free is free indeed." Your counselees can believe it! They should stand on God's Word and begin to think of godly things like the Apostle Paul warns us to do in Philippians 4:8. If you become worldly in your thinking, quote James 4:7, "Submit yourselves therefore to God and he will flee from you." By your counselees doing this and including God in their thought life during the day, they will be able to develop a very personal and intimate relationship with Jesus. Over time, your counselees' relationship with Jesus will replace the one they have with Satan. Your counselees may not realize they have a relationship with the devil, but examining the things that they think about is a good way to see who has the most influence in their life. As with all relationships, your counselees have to work at it; so now is the best time for them to start avoiding those evil thoughts and begin getting closer to Jesus. After all, He died on the Cross to save your counselees. Satan's only purpose is to destroy them.

NOTES:

1. The Talmud states that there are 613 commandments in the Torah, 248 Laws are positive and 365 Laws are negative, with an additional seven supporting laws legislated by the ancient rabbis of old which cover all aspects of Hebrew life. These Laws include male circumcision which, Paul argues, for a gentile to obey would make no sense" (Acts 15:1-10; Galatians 5:2-6). However, the Ten Commandments are the original Laws that God gave to Moses on Mount Sinai (Exodus 20:2-17) and traditionally, as Christians, we would only consider these Laws as the ones God intended for all of mankind.

2. *The 700 Club*, "Jason Illian." Produced by The Christian Broadcasting Network, July 19, 2005.

3. *The 700 Club*, "Andy Pettitte." Produced by The Christian Broadcasting Network, July 18, 2005.

CHAPTER 9

BIBLICAL SOLUTIONS
TO RESTORING VIRGINITY

As we previously mentioned in chapter 5, while Jesus was preaching at the Temple, some scribes and Pharisees brought a woman to Him they found committing adultery. Under the old covenant the penalty for extramarital sex was death. This was an attempt to entangle Jesus to make Him the judge who passed the death sentence on this unnamed woman,[1] thereby making Him responsible for her death. After all, Jesus had been positioning Himself in the eyes of the people as a great Rabbi, a great leader of morality. Jesus knew that extramarital sin went against God's Commandments. If He questioned them regarding exactly what they discovered her doing, all of the alleged and sordid details would become public; Jesus would have contributed to the titillation of the crowd that had gathered to hear Him preach. On the other hand, if Jesus passed judgment on her without detailing what she was accused of and allowed her to speak in her own defense, He would be guilty of the death of a possibly innocent person. If Jesus conducted a mini-trial, He would have set Himself above the legal authorities governing such procedures. It would seem that Jesus and the woman were both in a predicament.

Jesus kept a cool head and methodically wrote in the sand; after a few moments, He looked up and addressed her accusers. Knowing that the penalty of the Law for sex outside of marriage was death by stoning and because Jesus believed in justice according to the Law, He conceded that the penalty for such actions was death by stoning. However, He added one reservation: "He that is without sin among you, let him first cast a stone at her" (John 8:7b). The goal of the Pharisees was to put this woman to death; the goal of the woman was to save her body from death; the goal of Jesus was to save her soul. Her accusers slowly left, one by one, and this woman's life was restored to her. It makes us want to stand up and cheer! The Pharisees were foolish to attempt to put God in a trap. We can almost sense the tension that was in the air. This woman was just minutes from death, but she was saved by this stranger. Her head must have been spinning. Could it be that just a few moments before she was in the embrace of a man participating in a sinful sexual relationship, only to have been discovered, embarrassed, shocked and then fearfully bound and led toward a huge group of people with her accusers demanding that she be killed? Was a moment of passion worth a climax of death? Who was this stranger? He was like no one she had ever known. He saved her life and when He told her to go, she turned slowly and walked away, only to hear the stranger call out—she turned, looked once again into His piercing eyes as He said, probably with a smile on His lips, "Sin no more." He let her know that her sins had been forgiven, but not to take it for granted. Jesus understands how easy it is to make self-centered choices to satisfy our sinful fleshly lusts, but He also made it clear to this woman that a willful continuation in that sinful lifestyle was not acceptable!

The woman caught in adultery was never named in Scripture, but we see another unnamed woman in Luke 7 who, although not invited, entered the home of a Pharisee who was entertaining Jesus. She silently went in, opened a very expensive alabaster jar of ointment, and began to apply the ointment while washing Jesus' feet with her hair and tears. Her tears were not from fear, but from a devoted gratitude and loving affection. Perhaps this was the same woman Jesus saved from stoning. Whether or not it was the same woman, it is not implied anywhere in Scripture that there was any continuation of sexual misconduct after these encounters with Jesus.

Why did this change take place in them? The truth is apparent. These unnamed women decided that serving Jesus' needs was more important than serving their own needs. They wanted to do what Jesus wanted them to do, not what their fleshly desires wanted.[2]

Your counselees may think that doing what Jesus wants for their lives means that they cannot have any fun. Have them consider this: If those women continued doing what they thought of as fun, there would be a good possibility that they would be caught again, but Jesus may not have been in the area to help them. Fortunately for them, they learned their lesson and realized they wanted to follow Him. The result was personal satisfaction and because they truly repented, their sins were forgiven, their lives were no longer in danger, and their virginity was restored. The restoration of their virginity gained them great respect, admiration and favor in their communities. Were their lives better? Of course! Had they continued their lives as harlots, their lives would just have been untold stories of history, unknown and having little value and possibly eventually being stoned to death by the Pharisees. Today, two thousand years later, the story of these harlots has gained fame, respect and the admiration of believers throughout the world.

Many people, when afraid or caught in a sinful act, become momentarily repentant. However, the true measure of repentance is seen when we completely, not temporarily, turn from our wicked ways and proceed in a godly direction. This does not mean that temptations will cease; but if we are in Christ, it is not satisfaction that follows the sin but revulsion instead. The fruit of repentance is being repelled by sin and an ongoing struggle against it.

The woman who had a bad reputation and washed Jesus' feet with her tears is a wonderful role model for women and men alike. Her story shows that people can change, that old habits can be put off, and positive new habits can replace them. There is hope through the story of this woman for your counselee. No matter what their sins are and no matter what lifestyles they have slipped into, they can become new creatures through Christ. "Therefore if any man be in Christ, he is a new creature: old things are passed away; behold, all things are become new" (2 Corinthians 5:17).

<u>Establishing a Foundation</u>

How can you help your counselees change if they have no concept of right or wrong? By whose or by what standards do we use a measuring stick against the morality of our own lives? In chapter 2, we addressed the worldly pressures that invade all of our lives. The societal acceptance of recreational sex and the game of "changing partners" is much like the children's game, musical chairs. Children are taught in some schools that there are no moral absolutes and what applies to one may not be valid for another. They are taught that we live in a world of choices, and who is to say which choice is correct and which choice is not? In this world of clouded moral truths, the world becomes gray.[3] There is no moral compass, there is no standard, and there is no hope. Not even religion is exempt from this onslaught of non-truth.

At the end of the 18th century, the Bible came under scrutiny and ridicule. It began in Germany and was called "Higher Criticism." Only through the work of archaeologists who have documented biblical truth, along with believing biblical scholars, have the slings and arrows of those who criticize Christianity and Judaism been proven wrong. In keeping with this attack on God, a few decades later, Charles Darwin put forth his theory of the evolution of life having its genesis in a primordial swamp with common ancestry for all living things. In fact, the old saying, "Well, I'll be a monkey's uncle," is a direct result of such thinking. Contrary to the biblical vindication through science, the theory of evolution (which is taught in our public schools as fact) has not been vindicated. They have not found any transcending (connecting) fossils between species, not even one! While evolutionists *believe* solely in "naturalism" and insist that life must proceed from life and not from a Creator, to their great embarrassment, they do have to allow for one supernatural event, which is the miraculous appearance of (in their opinion) the very first life form, the lowly little anaerobic bacterium which appeared out of nothing at the very beginning of their so-called tree of life. Therefore, evolutionism is just as much a faith-based *religion* as theism. This, however, does not stop the thought police, the politically correct crowd and the tenor of our government schools in general.

Children are growing up without any commitment to the one and only true God, Jesus, because that would mean they are still living in the dark ages. Peer pressure and ridicule in school are strong taskmasters. Many children and young people we have talked with, who claim they are Christians, have no idea why they believe in Christ and upon closer scrutiny, display such ignorance of the Bible that they cannot defend themselves against even the simplest attacks on Christ. The new morality, being a matter of one's own opinion and thoughts, is rooted in the concept of *values' clarification*, but this doctrine of *values' clarification* does not clear up anything and leaves our society adrift in a sea of fog.

In her book, *Going All the Way*,[4] Sharon Thompson makes the observation that most teenage pregnancies are never planned. When questioning one girl about why she had sex, the typical answer came back that she did not really mean to have sex. She was just at a party and there was this cute guy. One thing led to another, and it happened. Do young people really think long-term? Generally, the concept of anticipating the results of our actions and the long-term repercussions created by individual acts does not begin to be considered in our thinking process until we are more mature. Most teenagers live for the moment and cannot think past the next test in school or their date on Friday. We have all been there.

Thompson relates the attitude of one girl she counseled who is fairly typical of young people today. A teenage mother just assumed that getting pregnant and having periods were just consequences of puberty. This unwed mother never considered the concept of virginity or what it would mean to lose it.

This is all too true for most of us today — young and old. Holiness and virginity (both being *set apart*) have become *old-fashioned* terms applied to some distant "goodie goodie" age of the past. In today's *enlightened* secular world, restricting rules are looked upon in our "free society" as not being avant-garde or cool.

As we stated, this thinking applies to the young and old alike. In the case of Claudia, the middle-aged Hollywood studio executive, she found herself surrounded by the trendsetters of the world's society. Many of the productions she worked on typically included sex, violence and rock-'n-roll. The concept of losing her virginity was not at the forefront of her mind, much less having any concern of offending a Holy God, nor was it on the mind of any of her associates. Yet, she was troubled when the aspect of premarital sex kept assaulting her.

She knew something was wrong, and she was troubled by the casual callousness of her dates who assumed they would have sex sometime during the evening. Something deep within told her this was wrong.[5] Sex, like a box of candy, is delicious for the moment, but when we step on the scales a few days later, we are shocked to see why we can no longer fit into our clothes. (Refer to Claudia's case history in chapter 5.)

Claudia, like many men and women, find themselves married, sexually active and then divorced. They have tasted the delights of the flesh and find themselves craving more. The fact that someone is divorced is a supposed green light that tells the world, "Been there, done that sexually." It is a signal to potential dates that this person is *sophisticated* and ready for more sex. Unfortunately, social pressures make it difficult for someone who does not agree with this train of thought to continue dating and be chaste. Most people just give up and go along with the way of the world. There is hope, and people do change! Chastity is not old-fashioned. God's Word is always up-to-date.

As the Apostle John writes, "In the beginning was the Word, and the Word was with God, and the Word was God" (John 1:1). In this passage, John is referring to Jesus and establishes that Jesus is both God and the Word. Scripture is also referred to as the Word of God. It is God's literal Word given to us through the divine inspiration of God the Holy Spirit. We are also told in Hebrews 13:8 that Jesus (who is the Word) is the same yesterday, today and tomorrow. Therefore, when we seek the Bible as our guide for morality, it is as up-to-date as any *sophisticated* publication on the market. It is far superior to any thinking of today's scholars, regardless of their degrees. God affirms that His "... thoughts are not your thoughts, neither are your ways my ways, says the LORD" (Isaiah 55:8). For this reason, it is beneficial for us to consistently apply God's Word to our lives.

The only way your counselees can succeed in changing is by accepting Jesus Christ as their Lord and Savior. Unfortunately, we have come to rely solely upon the sinner's prayer which basically requires us to repent of our sins, acknowledge that Jesus is the Son of God, that He died on the Cross for our salvation, and through acceptance of Him as our Lord and Savior, we are guaranteed eternal salvation. While this is an excellent beginning, salvation requires commitment. The sinner's prayer is not a magic spell that your counselees proclaim and then forget about. Your counselees need to understand that when they make a covenant or commitment, whether to the Lord, a job, school work, music lessons or to a family member, it commitment that requires their dedication. Commitment is accepting responsibility; it is not something you can shrug off; you must work at it. Commitment is also a lifelong experience of bettering ourselves by learning from our mistakes and trying not to repeat them again: that includes sinful mistakes. We are not saved by works, as Paul cautions, lest any man should boast (Ephesians 2:8-9), but we are to work out our salvation (Philippians 2:12) as we discussed in chapter 8 where counselees learned that they are to struggle against sin with constant efforts to please God who gave so much and asked so little.

With this in mind, your counselees should now be ready to commit themselves to a life of virtue and virginity, not because they have to, but because they love God so much that pleasing Him becomes more important than pleasing their own lustful desires. Think about it. "We love Him because He first loved us" (1 John 4:19), and He has loved us since the beginning of time even though we (mankind) have ignored Him and keep sinning against Him! Once your counselees understand this concept and a right relationship is formed between them and God, a virgin heart is not far behind. Submission to God is always joyful.

NOTES:
1. The gospels give us several examples about events that revolve around unnamed women of questionable morals. Although no names are given to these women, the events are so profound that virtually everyone knows about them. The myth that the prostitute was Mary Magdalene began through a sermon

given by Pope Gregory I in 591 AD. The Mary Magdalene in the gospels was a troubled woman who Jesus delivered from seven demons. Mary was so grateful that she became a loyal follower of Jesus and was present the morning of His resurrection (Matthew 27:56, 61; 28:1; Mark 15:40-41; 47; Mark 16:1, 9; Luke 8:2; 24:10; John 19:25; 20:1, 18).

2. Galatians 5:16 states, *"This* I say then, walk in the Spirit, and you shall not fulfill the lusts of the flesh."

3. David F. Wells, *Losing Our Virtue* (Grand Rapids: William B. Eerdmans Publishing Company, 1998), 60. Wells cites statistics that show 67% of Americans reject moral absolutes while 70% do not believe in relative or enduring absolutes. Therefore, the new standard of tolerance has been manifested and has become an oxymoron while allowing for tolerance of all views, opinions and lifestyles. They are absolutely intolerant about those who disagree with their view on tolerance.

4. Sharon Thompson, *Going All The Way* (New York: Hill and Wang, 1995), 113.

5. Claudia is who I would refer to as a "Veneer Christian." On the surface, these "Christians" know God and have accepted Jesus as their Lord and Savior, but are not committed or involved in a Bible-teaching church. Most of them are likely to attend church only on Christmas and Easter; but Claudia felt compelled to act in a moral way based upon what little Scriptures she knew. She derived what she believed as right and wrong mainly from the Ten Commandments. She knew her salvation was because Jesus died on the Cross for her sins; and because she believed in Him and His resurrection, she considered herself saved, a true believer and a Christian. The Holy Spirit convicted her heart based on her knowledge of the Ten Commandments, and she knew that what she was encountering was not morally pleasing to God. She would not have counseled with me had she not been under conviction. Hosea 4:6 tells us that God's people are destroyed for lack of knowledge. To strengthen your counselees' knowledge and commitment, have them set aside a daily time to develop and strengthen their personal relationship with Jesus.

CHAPTER 10

TAKING RESPONSIBILITY

As we have stated before, it is easy for your counselees to fail. They can find many excuses to forgive themselves for not succeeding, but there is only one excuse for success; that is to stick with it until they succeed, never allowing defeat to be permanent and never giving into feelings of failure. Success is just that—succeeding is goal-setting and accomplishing those goals. If they want to fail, it is easy. Failure is lack of effort. If they want to succeed, they must follow through with our commitments. Success is rewarded by their efforts. No one is ever imprisoned in the past; no one is ever bound to their present circumstance(s). God gave us free will, only in the sense of following our nature, which means we have the ability to alter our reality with His enablement, not through psychobabble, which ultimately ends in failure, but in victory through Christ Jesus who provides a way out for us. "There is no temptation taken you but such as is common to man: but God is faithful, who will not suffer (allow) you to be tempted above that you are able; but will with the temptation also make a way to escape, that you may be able to bear it" (1 Corinthians 10:13, clarification ours).

One of the many excuses we hear over and over again is, "I couldn't help myself; I didn't really want to have sex, but it just happened!" Nothing just happens. We allow it to happen. In areas of extramarital sex, your counselees would have to allow themselves to be in a situation that offers stimulation, accessibility and privacy. This can be in the car, on a couch in a home or a soft lawn in some out of the way secluded place. Darkness is always an adversary against morality. Your counselees have control over who they are with and where they go. If your counselees know that they have a tendency to succumb to an attractive member of the opposite sex, they need to make other arrangements. Double dating with a "moral couple" can be an alternative to disaster. Choosing friends is extremely important. There is an old saying: "We are known by the company we keep." There is a lot of truth in this statement. It is important to seek an environment of friends who are committed to godly morality. The Bible states, "Be ye not unequally yoked together with unbelievers: for what fellowship hath righteousness with unrighteousness? And what communion hath light with darkness" (2 Corinthians 6:14).

Your counselees must take responsibility and be accountable for their actions. They must carefully choose their friends; even if that means breaking off relationships with people they have hung around with in the past. Your counselees must avoid hangouts that encourage immorality. They must shun looking for mates in bars. Your counselees must avoid movies that rely on sexual titillation and outright nudity to sell tickets. They must make use of entertainment events that are G-rated and leave them with a sense of being morally uplifted rather than guilty. As stated in the previous chapter, it is not important just to *feel* good. We cannot rely on *feelings* alone because *feelings* will betray us most of the time. Your counselees need to be intellectually rooted in a manner of that Jesus would be proud of, meaning their thoughts must be pleasing to the Lord. By doing these things, your counselees are more able to interact with members of the opposite sex to whom they are attracted. By your counselees carefully choosing who they are with, where they go and what they do based on biblical morality, they are allowing themselves a means of securing and preserving their virginity. This is a good way your counselees can avoid finding themselves in compromising situations.

Because the Creator of mankind understands His own design and how it operates (as well as what problems cause it to fail), we must go to the Bible for the answers on how to address the problems we face in life. There is nothing under the sun that is new or has not been dealt with in the past. While it is true that we live in a more technologically advanced world than it was in the days when the Bible was given to us, we still face the same temptations and struggles that have been around since the beginning of time.

While Samson had to deal with his lust for women, including the beautiful Delilah, men have problems in today's society dealing with beautiful Delilahs, tempting them on the Internet (and in person too—that has not gone away either). Lust is the same; only the medium has changed. Sin is sin, and lust for a beautiful human body is nothing new. The Bible, therefore, deals with all of the problems of the heart with which everyone struggles. Once your counselees have committed their lives to Jesus and acknowledged that they are sinners in need of a Savior, then and only then can the hope of change begin in their lives.

You must caution your counselees to be careful of "12-step" programs and other self-help courses and books. For a text to work, you must have faith that the authors know what they are talking about. They should always look for an author's credibility. For example, what degree(s) do they have? What is their professional background and experience? Is there an endorsement from a well-known and respected college included with their work? These are all important items to consider before anyone decides to purchase a book, follow its directions and apply them to the area(s) in which they need help. Your counselees should always be inquisitive about what program the designers are basing their agendas on (i.e., who and what they consulted). Most importantly, they must understand that there is no "one size fits all" program. Only the Bible holds *all* of the answers for dealing with *any* problem you may have, and it is filled with meaningful passages that can be tailored to each unique individual God created.

Biblical truths are facts and God's Laws apply to all of us without exception. What is true for the Christian is true for the unbeliever as well. If a person, saved or unsaved, lives their life according to the basic Ten Commandments of God, they will profit. The Bible teaches that truths are truths, regardless of whether or not someone acknowledges the existence of God. We read in Matthew, "That you may be the children of your Father which is in heaven: for He makes His sun to rise on the evil and on the good, and sends rain on the just and on the unjust" (Matthew 5:45). However, in order for serious problems to be addressed, your counselees need to believe that what they read in the Bible is true and that it comes from God who is all-knowing and all-wise. When we believe in God and His Word, great changes affect our lives. The Word is powerful and can change even the most difficult cases. The key factor in the use of Scripture is our faith and its life-changing power. To pick and choose only what you want to believe cancels out the power of God's Word. Your counselees must either completely accept the teachings of Scripture or completely reject them. They cannot accept only the teachings in the Bible that they agree with, while rejecting the warnings of sinful lifestyles because they enjoy that particular sin. In order for a healing to take place, your counselees have to avail themselves of the treatment that will cure it. Another way of saying this is that if you want to protect yourself from a certain disease, you have to submit yourself to the sting of a needle. In order to make life-changing commitments, sometimes there may be some pain involved. The Bible does not protect your counselees from pain, but it guarantees a healing.

Fortunately, the Bible is the textbook of life. The Bible is not necessarily a G-rated publication because it has stories of lust, murder, homosexuality, promiscuity, cunningness and paganism. Why does God allow so many X-rated stories in His Holy Word? He does not do this to titillate but to teach. When we read the stories in the Bible, we find people just like us—people who have fallen into various disgusting habits and sinful lifestyles. Through the Bible, God allows us to see the results firsthand of such corrupted living. In revealing many of these horrific stories, God also shows us a way out. With these glimpses into human nature, we find alternatives, we find instruction, and we find hope.

God does not hate people. In fact, He loves us so much that He prepared a way of escape from the problems that beset us all. "For God so loved the world, that He gave His only begotten Son, that whosoever believeth in Him should not perish, but have everlasting life" (John 3:16). Jesus is telling us in this passage that God loves everyone. No matter what we have done, God is bigger than our problems, if only we believe. What is belief? It is faith—a two-edged sword because it can cut both ways. Obviously, *God has enough faith in us* to recognize His message of hope; a message for a way out of our problems if *we only have faith in Him.*

There is no better text for life than the best selling book of all time—the Bible! Throughout the millenniums, the Bible has stood the test of time. The divinely-inspired collection of books it contains has done more to change the directions of nations and people than all other books combined. Its pedigree is indisputable, and its results are nothing short of miraculous. This is why the only consistently tried and true method of helping people is found in the life-changing teachings of the Scriptures.

Since we are dealing with virginity, your counselees must realize that by its very definition it is something *set apart*, easy to lose and hard to restore. Once someone has lost their virginity, the general belief is that they have lost it forever. The world will tell them that they are used goods, so they might as well continue in that lifestyle because once they have lost their virginity, they can never get it back. As we have seen, the truth is that restoring one's virginity is not impossible. Difficult—yes but not impossible. Jesus says, and this applies to restored virginity as well, that from the world's point of view "… this is impossible but with God all things are possible" (Matthew 19:26). Could your counselees have any better assurance than this, coming from the mouth of God's own Son who healed the sick, raised the dead and made the blind to see?

Our case studies show that some men and women were able, through commitment, faith and hard work, to restore what was lost. The Bible makes it clear that man is sinful by nature and because of this, it was necessary for Jesus to come to save the lost. If something is not precious, losing it means nothing. Many times we have lost something and because we did not value it, we did not realize it was gone until years later. Your counselees' purity is very special. Virginity is a commitment to save themselves for the exclusiveness of the person they will marry someday. To lose it just for the sake of recreation means to put no value on it. Therefore, its loss means nothing to them. When your counselees realize the sinful mistake they have made and regrets having been so free to share it in a casual way, the value of what they lost becomes serious. The good news is that through Jesus, they can restore what was lost (Matthew 18:11).

How do your counselees do it? They do it by committing to a way of life that is pleasing to God in order that they may be blessed. Once your counselees focus on pleasing God instead of themselves, it is only a matter of time before they reach their goal. Counselees are usually concerned with failure and wonder if it is possible that they might fail at first. Of course, that is a real possibility, but they must realize that we all fail, but only those who get discouraged and give up cannot and do not succeed.

A Practical Biblical Exercise
to Help You Begin
Restoring Your Virginity

On the following pages are some Scriptures that have been found to help people turn their lives around and free themselves from sexual sin. Have your counselees memorize them and even apply them for their situation when they pray. They may also find it very beneficial to personalize them when they talk with God or when they are confronting sexual temptation.

One of the things counselees can do when they are tempted to sin is mentally shift gears and start walking down what I personally refer to as "my prayer path." My prayer path consists of recalling certain Scriptures in an order that flows in a meaningful way. This will not only encourage your counselees, but also help get their minds focused on something godly as opposed to thinking on those sinful temptations. By distracting their minds from lustful thoughts, they are able through the Word of God to crowd out thoughts that cause us to sin. This can be part of your goal-setting as well. Below is a practical exercise for your counselees to work on that is very similar to the type of prayer path that I walk down with Jesus when I am tempted. As your counselees are looking up those Scriptures and filling in the blanks, they are not alone on this path, but walking hand-in-hand with Jesus. Sometimes they may even think of Jesus putting his arm around them as they go down the prayer path together.

"God, I'm afraid I can't be freed from my sexual desires. Is there any hope for me? It seems so impossible for me to get control of my lustful *feelings* and thoughts that I wonder if even You can help me overcome my sexual cravings."

Jesus has the answer for you. Look up Matthew 19:26.

_____

_____

_____

_____

That is encouraging, but how do I go about changing? (John 8:32)

_____

_____

_____

_____

Jesus, I want to know the truth but I don't know the way, help me. (John 14:6)

_____

_____

_____

_____

_____

Jesus, why is it that I am so drawn to my sins? (John 8:34)

_____

_____

_____

_____

Can I really be set free? How can I be assured that I am? (John 8:36)

_____

_____

_____

_____

Does that mean I can really have my virginity restored after I have been sexually active? (2 Corinthians 5:17)

_____

_____

_____

_____

_____

Jesus, will you come into my heart and strengthen me always? (Philippians 4:13)

_____

_____

_____

_____

(and 1 John 4:4b)

_____

_____

_____

_____

Lord, how can I resist Satan? Do I just cast him out in Your name or how do I do it? (James 4:7)

_____

_____

_____

_____

_____

Once your counselees have memorized these Scriptures, they can apply them to their lives when temptation gets in their way.

An example of a practical application is John 8:32 when your counselees are tempted. "I know the truth. Jesus is setting me free from pornography, and that truth has made me free from sexual sin!"

Perhaps your counselees are tempted to engage in sexual intercourse. They should think about Philippians 4:13. "I don't have to engage in sex now, even though my body really wants me to because 'I can do all things through Christ which strengthens me.' Jesus is in me and He promises to give me the strength to stop; I will not make Him a liar!" Then your counselees should remove themselves quickly from the situation they are in that is compromising him and his girlfriend or her with her boyfriend. Counselees should never buy into Satan's old lie which is, "Do it now and ask forgiveness later." The Bible warns against this type of thinking. "What shall we say then? Shall we continue in sin, that grace may abound? God forbid. How shall we, that are dead to sin, live any longer therein" (Romans 6:1-2)? Paul writes, "Be not deceived; God is not mocked (do not sin and ask for forgiveness later) for whatsoever a man sows, that shall he also reap. For he that sows to his flesh shall of the flesh reap corruption (AIDS and other sexually transmitted diseases); but he that sows to the Spirit shall of the Spirit reap life everlasting" (Galatians 6:7-8, clarification ours).

Repetition is the key to success, so below we have once again laid out those Scriptures we recommend that your counselees learn and apply to their lives. While chosen especially with men in mind, these Scriptures are just as powerful for women too. Perhaps you may have some other Scriptures that you will want your counselees to look up and memorize. The more your counselees think on and internalize these verses, the less they will allow themselves to think sinful thoughts. I like to think that I am filling up my heart with the Word of God and by doing this, I am crowding out the sinful thoughts that I have allowed to fester and grow. Encourage your counselees to get a Bible that is easy for them to understand and that has a good concordance in the back.

When temptation starts to lead your counselees into sexually compromising activities or thoughts that can drag them back into sin, they now have the Word of God tucked away inside their hearts which allows them to more firmly stand their ground and be able to claim, "I'm free from that stuff. Why would I want to get involved with *that* again? I'M NOT GOING THERE!" They can now change their focus to the Scriptures they have memorized and keep reciting them. Keep your counselees standing on them over and over again until the temptation has passed. They can now have victory through Christ, but they must also take some of the responsibility themselves. "Submit yourselves therefore to God. Resist the Devil, and he will flee from you" (James 4:7)!

On the next pages your counselees will find some Scriptural applications to feed their hearts as they begin restoring their virginity.

Scriptures to Keep a
Virgin Mind in a Virgin Body

(The following Scriptures are taken from the NIV Bible, modification ours)

Scriptures in dealing with pornography and pornographic thoughts:

Psalm 101:2-3

I, (name here), will be careful to lead a blameless life—when will You (God) come to me? I will walk in my house with a blameless heart. I (name here) will set before my eyes no vile (pornographic) thing. The deeds of faithless men I hate; they will not cling to me (i.e., I will not associate myself with bad influences [clarification ours]).

James 4:7-8

Submit yourself, (name here), to God. Resist the devil, and he will flee from you. Come near to God, (name here), and He will come near to you. Wash your hands, you sinners, and purify your hearts, you double-minded.

James 1:8

A double-minded man is unstable in all his ways (KJV).

Philippians 4:8

Finally, (name here), whatever is true, whatever is noble, whatever is right, whatever is pure, whatever is lovely, whatever is admirable— if anything is excellent or praiseworthy—think about such things.

Scriptures to help you keep from acting out sexually either with someone or through masturbation:

Luke 1:37
For with God, (name here), nothing shall be impossible (KJV).

John 14:6
Jesus Himself promises to me: "I am the way and the truth and the life. No one comes to the Father except through Me."

John 8:32
Then, (name here), will know the truth, and the truth will set *me* free.

John 8:34
Jesus replies, "I tell you the truth, (name here), everyone who sins is a slave to sin.

John 8:36
So, (name here), if the Son sets you free, you will be free indeed (and I receive it!).

2 Corinthians 5:17
Therefore, if (name here) is in Christ, he is a new creation; the old has gone, the new has come!

Philippians 4:13
I, (name here), can do all things through Christ which strengthens me (KJV).

Scriptures to encourage you not to participate in sexual joking, flirting or sexual innuendos

Ephesians 4:29
Do not let any unwholesome talk come out of your mouth, (name here), but only what is helpful for building others up according to their needs, that it may benefit those who listen (clarification ours).

Ephesians 5:4

(Name here), let: "Neither filthiness, nor foolish talking, nor jesting, which are not convenient: but rather giving of thanks" (KJV).

Matthew 12:34

You brood of vipers, how can you who are evil say anything good? **For out of the overflow of the heart the mouth speaks** (emphasis ours).

Scriptures to remind you to not give up, but keep standing and applying God's Word to restore and maintain your virginity.

2 Corinthians 13:5

Examine yourselves, (name here), to see whether you are in the faith; test yourselves. Do you not realize that Christ Jesus is in you—unless, of course, you fail the test?

1 John 1:8-9

If we say that we have no sin, we deceive ourselves, and the truth is not in us. If we confess our sins, He is faithful and just to forgive us our sins, and to cleanse us from all unrighteousness (KJV).

1 Corinthians 6:9-10

Do you not know, (name here), that the wicked will not inherit the kingdom of God? Do not be deceived: Neither the sexually immoral nor idolaters nor adulterers nor male prostitutes nor homosexual offenders nor thieves nor the greedy nor drunkards nor slanderers nor swindlers will inherit the kingdom of God.

1 Corinthians 10:13

There is no temptation taken you, (name here), but such as is common to man: but God is faithful, who will not allow you to be tempted above that ye are able; but will with the temptation also make a way to escape, that ye may be able to bear it (KJV clarification ours).

CHAPTER 11

CONCUBINAGE: AMERICA'S NEW LIFESTYLE

With the dawning of the twenty-first century, the demographics of cohabiting couples versus married couples dramatically shifted. Without realizing it, American women are subjecting themselves to becoming lowly concubines in the literal since of the word as we will see later. After a steady increase in couples living together without the benefit of marriage, the scales finally tipped in favor of the cohabiting couples toward the end of 2006. Statistics show that there are more unmarried couples living together than married couples, and the trend is steadily increasing. The statistics for this report also included homosexual couples which, traditionally, was never a valid consideration before.[1]

In this chapter, we will discuss a serious societal phenomenon, the return of the concubine. It is a topic that we did not bring up in our companion book, *You Can Be a Virgin Again,* because many of today's youth may resist or find it difficult to fully comprehend. Therefore, we believe you are better able to address this sinfully demeaning trend with your counselees through a more sensitive and appropriate manner than we could have done in our companion book. Concubinage has not changed throughout history. Instead, it has only recently become redefined and acceptable through our modern trend of living together outside of marriage.

The so-called battle of the sexes has always been around, from Adam and Eve up to and including the present time. However, with the Feminist Movement of the 1960s and forward, women have been duped into thinking that they should behave as men. This includes swearing, sleeping around without any commitment, being in traditionally male-held jobs such as military warriors, operating heavy equipment on construction sites, police officers and fire fighters, the right to eliminate an inconvenient pregnancy anytime they want, living together outside the sanctity of marriage, drinking and carousing and even more aggressive—criminal behavior all in the name of equal rights!

Also, in the 1960s the A.C.L.U., along with an activist United States Supreme Court, the onslaught against God began in our society. As they progressed, the goal of removing any vestige of God and the Ten Commandments from our society has been relentless. The 1960s moral rebellion and couples living together without the sanctity of marriage became more and more socially acceptable. Before, where couples had to be married in order to get a motel room, rent an apartment, and buy a home has now since been deemed unconstitutional and has opened the way for unrestrained cohabitation. In the 1990s, homosexual couples began demanding the same benefits as married couples; government employers began to accommodate them with industries complying soon afterward. Now heterosexual couples are living together without the benefit of marriage and demanding the same *equal rights* as the homosexual couples who began receiving marriage benefits without marriage as well. With all of this added together with the lack of a marriage tax penalty, it was not long before people began to realize that you could live together and benefit financially more than if you were legally married. You can now have all of the benefits without all of the hassle and if you get tired of living together, you just move on. When it comes to parting ways, this is great for the men, but for the women it is a different matter. In our throw away society, women are the ones who benefit the least because they are usually left out in the street with nothing to show for it when their services are no longer wanted or needed.

It is very sad that women think after thousands of years of struggling in the battle of the sexes that they have finally achieved equality with men. By what measure are they equal to men? We would submit that the only thing the Feminist Movement has attained for women is sinking to the lowest level of the negative attributes of men. So now they have bragging rights that they can be as filthy, demeaning, crass and promiscuous s as any guy. In the words of an old cigarette commercial, "You've come a long way baby," but in the wrong direction.

In the feminist movement, marriage is considered a form of slavery and demeaning to women. They consider the Bible as having been written by a bunch of patriarchal, domineering old men from a chauvinistic failed society of a bygone era. Today's women are now finally free. Free from what, free to do what, one may ask? They are free to return to an archaic demeaning condition that relegates them to a status of a modern concubine! *Random House Webster's College Dictionary* defines concubinage as, "1) a woman who cohabits with a man to whom she is not legally married." Furthermore, this same dictionary defines a concubine the same way.[2]

Some may argue that we are being too harsh by saying that women who are living with "their significant other" are living in sin and are a concubine. However, as we have shown throughout this book, living together without the benefit of marriage is biblically living in sin, and by its very definition relegates the woman from the potentially high status of a wife to the inferior place of a concubine. Yes, it is demeaning, but only because the Feminist Movement has not only looked upon cohabitation with approval but, has encouraged it as a preferred arrangement as well, much to the detriment of the hapless women.

While it is true that concubines are mentioned in the Bible and many of our biblical heroes, such as King David and Solomon, had many wives and concubines, *nowhere* in the Bible do we find that God approves of such an arrangement. Think about the Tenth Commandment. "You shall not covet your neighbor's house. You shall not covet your neighbor's wife, or his manservant or maidservant, his ox or donkey, or anything that belongs to your neighbor" (Exodus 20:17, NIV). Notice what it does *not* say. It does not say, "You shall not covet your neighbor's house. You shall not covet *any of your neighbor's wives or concubines ....*" When God created Adam and Eve, He created them man and wife (Genesis 2:24-25). From the start, God did not create them Adam, Eve and concubine. We can see the problems with having more than one wife as well as a man taking a concubine for himself, which is basically a woman who prostitutes her body and services to one man in exchange for the lowly role of a common concubine. Does this elevate a woman's status in a man's eyes? Does it elevate her status in a positive way? Can a woman feel valued by the one she loves without a commitment of marriage? Is her relationship more secure as a concubine as opposed to the legal status of being wed? Legally, it is far more costly and difficult to get any legal satisfaction from a man who has no lawful commitment if he abandons her or tells her to leave. In addition to Genesis 2:25 where God created marriage to be between one man and one wife, He also tells men that if they wish to serve Him they should be the husband of one wife (1 Timothy 3:1).

We had the pleasure to be acquainted with a very well known and much beloved American pastor. He shared how some of his pastor friends counseled him after his wife died not to remarry, but to find a "concubine" instead. To this wonderful pastor's credit, he rejected their counsel and later married a wonderful woman he honored and loved. Why would someone, especially a pastor, advise someone else to "take a concubine" rather than to marry? To be kind, perhaps it was just an eisegetical (reading into Scripture something that it does not say) biblical interpretation.

A brief overview of concubinage is found throughout history, usually with kings and the wealthy aristocracy. Because it takes money to maintain a household, much less one with several wives and concubines, it was only feasible for men of great wealth and power to indulge themselves in that manner. Therefore, throughout history having many wives and concubines was limited to kings and the very affluent. It was also looked upon as a position of status as well as for conjugal indulgence. Sometimes kings gave their daughters to other kings as wives to solidify treaties between their kingdoms.

This is how King Solomon acquired some of his wives (1 Kings 3:1), but a royal princess would never be given as a concubine. In time, as babies were born to their daughters, the royal bloodlines became strengthened through their newly produced children. Through the creation of paternal and maternal grandparents, peaceful coexistence between kingdoms was reinforced. King Solomon had seven hundred wives and three hundred concubines (1 Kings 11:2-3). The status of women in a royal court (or a potentate's household) was usually in the order of the favorite wife first (usually the youngest and prettiest), the lesser wives second (the ones who had fallen out of favor), and the third or lowest class fell to the concubine(s).

One of the earliest recorded biblical incidents of a man taking a concubine is found in the book of Genesis in chapter 16. This story revolves around the Hebrew Patriarch, Abraham. We covered this story in chapter 4, but for the sake of argument let us revisit it one more time in the light of concubinage. Abraham and his wife, Sarah, were getting up in age and Sarah was barren. Because they believed God's promise that Abraham would be the father of many people, Sarah thought they could *help* God fulfill His promise through the socially accepted practice of the time which was for Sarah to offer her hand maid, Hagar, as a concubine for her husband, Abraham. Because there was no peer pressure against doing such a thing and "everyone was doing it," Abraham consented to the scheme. Hagar bore Abraham a son, but soon Abraham's concubine started making trouble for Sarah (vv. 4-5). Here is the interesting point. Sarah was becoming very old while Hagar was still youthful. However, Abraham did not have the option to choose between his attractive young concubine and his aging wife because, as Jesus Himself said when questioned about marriage and divorce by the Pharisees:

> Haven't you read, He replied, that at the beginning the Creator 'made them male and female,' and said, 'For this reason a man will leave his father and mother and be united to his wife, and the two will become one flesh?' So they are no longer two, but one. Therefore what God has joined together, let man not separate (Matthew 19:4-6, NIV).

Consequently, Abraham had to honor his wife's wishes because God ordained their marriage; but Hagar, his concubine, was another matter. So it was that Abraham allowed his wife, Sarah, to send his concubine and her son away. Notice the pecking order and who it was in the end that supplanted Abraham's concubine. It was Sarah who was victorious because of her exalted position as Abraham's wife. It was this status that dictated the outcome of events, much to the chagrin of the lowly concubine. Abraham could have spared himself and his wife, Sarah, a lot of trouble and grief if he had not strayed from God's plan of marriage between one man and one wife. It is no different today. When a man gets tired of his wife, it is not an easy matter to dissolve their mutual commitment of marriage; but when it is only a live-in lover (i.e., a concubine), casting her aside is "no big deal." Sadly, for the so-called liberated women of today who are living with their "boyfriends," "fiancés," or "significant others," only the words they use to justify their living arrangement have changed, but the inescapable status of being a concubine is still the same.

It would be good to reflect here for a moment that if a man takes one concubine, what is to prevent him from having a second or a third concubine or even more—all at the same time? Having more than one wife is illegal, but there is no law regarding cohabitation. Consider the fact that having a concubine requires no legally binding agreement one way or the other and if a man chooses to have several concubines around town or around the country, who would know and what is to stop him?

Sadly, for the woman nothing has changed since Abraham's day. As we documented at the beginning of this chapter, a woman who cohabits with a man she is not legally married to is nothing more than a concubine and to make matters worse, she is sinning against God by doing so. To deny that fact, our so-called liberated women are only fooling themselves. Welcome to the American concubinage of the twenty-first century!

The more things change the more they remain the same.

NOTES:
1. United States Census Bureau Report, October, 2006 reveals that less than half (49.7%) of all couples living together in the United States of America now are actually legally married.
2. *Random House Webster's College Dictionary*, s.v. (1990), "Concubinage," "concubine."

CHAPTER 12

CAUTIONS IN COUNSELING

In the previous case histories we discussed, we observed people who were caught up in sex outside of marriage. Each case is unique. No two people or their situations are ever exactly the same. In chapter 5, Shannon dealt with some of the unique problems that arose and discussed ways of addressing those problems on a one-by-one basis. Counselors must be very careful to never *assume* that there is a "magic" formula that can be applied to similar problems. This is a trap into which both secular and Christian counselors fall. After years of helping people, we get into the habit of using clichés and methods that generally seem to work.

However, since no two people are alike, although some may resemble each other very closely in certain ways, every human heart is different. The counselor must be on guard at all times to listen intently to what their counselees are actually saying and implying. This means that sometimes people will say one thing while really hinting at something else. It is the job of the counselor to discern between a smoke screen and a cry for help.

We once talked with a man who was the best salesman in his field. He told us that unsuccessful salesmen get easily discouraged when they run into roadblocks when a customer brings up negatives. Some of the negatives salespeople encounter are things like, "Well, I've heard this widget always breaks down after so many hours of running time," or, "I've heard the material that this widget is made out of tends to break easily," or, "I heard that So and So makes a better widget than yours and it's a lot cheaper." These types of arguments from the customer intimidate some salespeople, so much that they give up trying to sell their product because they assume the customer is just a negative person trying to give them a hard time.

The truth of the matter, our friend tells us, is that the customer really wants to buy his widget, and the negative comments he is bringing up are just smoke screens. In reality, they *want* their objections shot down by you because they really want what you have to offer. It is just that they need to be assured by a convincing argument that what you have to offer is the *real thing*. The customer is actually saying, "I like your product, but I am nervous about spending so much money because other salesmen and people have told me that your product may not be all that I want it to be. If you can convince me they are wrong, I'll buy your widget today."

The point we are making is that the counselor must not be put off by some of the negatives or apparent lack of interest on the part of the counselee. To begin with, the counselee would not be sitting across from you if he were not at least, at some level, really desiring your help. Your job is to find the perceived objections that he wants *you* to overcome so that he can invest himself in what you have to offer. What is it you have to offer as a counselor? The answer is simple—HOPE—hope that the counselee can change from the person he is to the person he wants to be.

Where do we begin? For a person to achieve a monumental change in his life, he must divest himself of preconceived ideas and be willing to allow change to take place. In order to do this, he cannot look to himself because the heart is evil and filled with madness (Ecclesiastes 9:3). When the light of truth shines upon their hearts, they either melt or become hard. In order to have your counselees' hearts changed for the good; they must be willing to seek help from the One who made it in the first place (Psalm 51:10).

It can never be stressed enough how important it is to find out where the counselees stand in regard to the salvation issue. The counselees cannot be *saved* from their troubles if they do not have a *Savior*. Generally speaking, with a few exceptions, the problems in people's lives are caused by one of our natures, the one the Bible calls sin. Therefore, the counselees must face up to the fact that they have a problem with sin. In order to do this, the salvation issue must be addressed up front.

In today's world, secular counseling talks about "mental illness." This is an oxymoron since mental ethereal phenomena has no substance. That which has no substance cannot be diseased. A disease is something that is acquired by a bacterial or viral pathogen. While it is true that thoughts can be affected, the mind cannot be infected by a physical world.

However, there are instances when the brain, through trauma, lack of oxygen, hemorrhaging (stroke), epilepsy, diabetes, multiple sclerosis, hormonal shifts, etc., can manifest peculiar behavior in a person, but this is not mental illness. These are physical malfunctions and, as such, must be brought to the attention of a medical doctor and/or neurosurgeon. Purposeful preoccupation and acting out are physical manifestations of the heart (soul/spirit).

Too often we hear that people cannot help themselves because they are victims of their environment. This is a Rogerian concept, which, on the surface makes sense and appears logical; however, upon further study it becomes obvious that an individual is able to change his environment and seek counseling based upon scriptural wisdom that has the *power* to change lives. The Rogerian concept implies that the individual is helpless and a victim—that it is not his fault. The Bible teaches that we are responsible for our actions. We can overcome things that beset us and through Christ we can be set free (John 8:36).

Once the counselees have been presented the salvation message and have affirmed or accepted their relationship with Christ, then and only then are they able to receive life-changing instruction for their lives. To attempt to counsel those without their acknowledgment of Jesus Christ as their personal Lord and Savior would be futile, thus making it necessary to evangelize the counselees before beginning to address their particular problems.

Accepting Responsibility

We have all sinned and fallen short of the glory of God (Romans 3:23). Because of this, we cannot use the excuse that we are victims of our circumstances. Since we know that actions cause reactions according to Sir Isaac Newton, we must not allow that to become the source for permission to fail. Bad things happen to us all, as do good things, which we showed earlier in chapter 10 when we cited Matthew 5:45. Therefore, we must not allow ourselves to let the past govern our future. Today, many secular counselors seek to revisit the past and dig up events that can provide excuses for bad behaviors. The past no longer exists. We cannot change the past; we can only change our future. We live in the present, and this is the only reality of which we are assured. Yesterday is gone and tomorrow may never come. The question then becomes "What are we going to do now?"

While the past can become permission for sinful habits when we are older, patterns that have been established throughout the years and influences during our formative years can and do affect tendencies in one's life. Secularists are so convinced of the looming control in our lives from these past events that they have made entire careers out of allowing their counselees to feel good about themselves because it is these past events that are at fault for the counselee's present behavior. This doctrine holds the counselees innocent of their present situation by making them mere victims without any accountability by blaming their present failures on their past.

This is bogus at best; but there is a level of truth in acknowledging that behavioral patterns can be instilled during our formative years. In Proverbs we find, "Train up a child in the way he should go: and when he is old, he will not depart from it" (Proverbs 22:6). This is a warning that one must be systematic in the enforcement of the moral values that are observed from the time a child is born until the time the child leaves home. Of course, such dynamic influences will have an effect. A child who is reared in an ungodly home, even a broken home, and who faces abuse and condemnation on a daily basis will also show manifestations of his upbringing. Likewise, secularists who deal with children who have been sexually abused and continue independently as teenagers and young adults in a life of debauchery, blame their actions on their unfortunate backgrounds. What about those children from good backgrounds who have lost their virginity in their early teens and have continued in a lifestyle of promiscuity? In their case, the secularists say this is perfectly normal and they are just acting upon their natural animal instincts. This is simply disingenuous psychobabble because they want to have it both ways.

Biblical counselors know this is an excuse, if not an encouragement, for human beings to continue in a life of premarital sex. Contrary to the secularists, biblical counselors are aware that while people are created with many of the same types of organs and needs as animals (i.e., the need to breathe air, eat food, seek shelter, etc.), they have been created as a unique creature in the image of God (Genesis 1:26a).

People are not trapped by their pasts. They are not robots who have been programmed by a series of events over which they have no control. Sure, we make choices. We can even choose to reject God's free plan of salvation for us. The reason we are able to accept or reject our circumstances and our way of life is because we have been created with a free will and allowed to make life-altering choices as witnessed by the events of Genesis 3.

A Christian counselor will take into consideration all data gathering, including past traumatic events in the counselee's life, but the difference between biblical counselors and secular counselors is that biblical counselors know that through Christ, life-changing events can occur. We are not forever trapped in a lifestyle or socioeconomic prison because we have the ability to make choices that will enable us to make dramatic and positive changes in our lives. We are assured, "Therefore if any (hu)man *be* in Christ, *(s)he is* a new creature: old things are passed away; behold, all things are become new" (2 Corinthians 5:17, clarification ours). To claim that people are victims is a disservice to them and leaves no hope for change.

Biblically-based Christian counselors may look at the past, but must never allow it to be used as a cop-out for premarital sex or destructive *behavior of any sort.* It is important to realize that all bad behavior is rooted in sin, and who is better able to deal with sin than God?

Biblical Christian counseling is not based on opinions of human beings. It is based upon incorruptible facts that have been given to mankind by our Creator. As previously stated, it only makes sense that we take a car in need of repair to a mechanic, not to a gardener. The gardener may be a genius when it comes to nurturing plants and designing beautiful gardens, but a gardener's expertise is in another area. Likewise, when it comes to rebuilding a carburetor or a transmission, we would be wise to seek the advice of a factory-trained mechanic instead.

Unlike many secular psychologists who, in the manner of Carl Rogers, do their counseling sessions in a passive, non-confrontational and non-judgmental manner, biblical Christian counseling must be confrontational. It is because biblical counseling *must* by its very nature be confrontational because counselors cannot allow the counselee to dictate the counseling agenda. However, a word of caution is necessary. While confronting counselees, we must also express the love of Christ. Our confrontation must never be interpreted as aggressively hostile or demeaning. Some discouraged counselees have complained that their counselor conveyed a "better than Thou" attitude and seemed to always anticipate what the counselee was going to say rather than listening to them. This has been very discouraging and has led to counselees ending their counseling sessions. While we must not shy away from confronting sin, we must gently admonish the counselees with the accurate use of Scripture. By assigning homework that uses Scripture to address the very area of sin that the counselee is involved in, often the counselees discover on their own what the problem is while allowing the Word of God to bring about conviction to their heart. This can be a breakthrough with which the counselor can encouragingly build upon in follow-up sessions.

Remember, no two people are alike and each person should be treated on a case-by-case basis. We have warned that counselors must constantly be on guard to not fall into the trap of *assuming* that one case is so similar to another that it can be treated in the same manner. Having reaffirmed this, however, there are some basic guidelines which a counselor must follow in order to successfully outline a plan for productive counseling. Some of these basics will be discussed in the following outline.

First, we have discussed how a counselee must be evangelized in order for biblical counseling to have any success.

Second, after establishing the counselee's salvation issue, the next step is to address their history. This is usually done through a form the counselee completes before their first session (see Appendix A). It contains vital information which allows the counselor to get an overview of the counselee's problem area. The counselor must be cautious, however, not to accept all that the counselee has revealed because most people try to present themselves in the best light possible. It is the job of the counselor to see through any smoke screens or favorable positioning created by the counselee.

Third, it is important at the outset for the counselor to establish a candid and honest relationship with the counselee. A counselor must never become intimidated by the fear of insulting the counselee by his frankness, but should always confront in a loving Christ-like manner. The counselor should not be rude, but must be direct and in control of the conversation. The counselee expects to be treated with integrity by someone who has insight and experience in dealing with troubled people. The counselee also expects the counselor to be up front and honest with him. It is the job of the counselor to confront the counselee squarely with their problem. There is a difference between being firm and being rude and confronting as opposed to being confrontational. Sometimes it is a fine line to walk, but to be wishy-washy and afraid of speaking the truth because it may be offensive will never help the counselee with his problem. It is important to face head on, in love, the negative aspects of a person's life.

Fourth, while pointing out the counselee's sinful flaws, it is equally important to give them hope. It is hope that brought them to you in the first place. When one anticipates that he can be helped, he is in fact hoping for the best. The Bible offers that hope.

How do we know this? We must be able to offer the struggling counselees more than just a pat on the back and a few kind words. We must show them what God has to say about their issue(s), thus giving them hope.

Fifth, another important aspect of counseling on a person-by-person basis is to have the counselee commit to a lifestyle that edifies Christ along with implementing the biblical homework that has been assigned to them. Since we are involved with guiding the counselees to restoring their virginity, we must enact certain guidelines that will enforce a new way of living through step-by-step encouragement. Virginity is attainable. Your counselees must be encouraged that their desire to restore their virginity is a positive and attainable cause. They need to know that this is not a foolish desire, but a noble and godly quest that will allow them to once again attain that precious and godly virtue.

CONCLUSION

J esus understands our shortcomings, and came to save us because we are unable to save ourselves. When we fail the first time, Satan is always ready to tell us, "See, you can't do it. You're too weak." We must remember that Christ is the winner, and the enemy has already been defeated.

When we have accepted Jesus as our Lord and Savior, we become empowered to become the children of God (John 1:12). The Apostle John tells us, "You are of God, little children, and have overcome them: because greater is He that is in you, than he (Satan) that is in the world" (1 John 4:4, clarification ours).

Walter Elwell sums up the victory over sin, that is most applicable to the restoration of the counselees' virginity through Jesus Christ when he states, "The saving act of God in Christ alone rectifies this dilemma. Only by the complete work of Jesus, the God-man, can God's righteousness become man's." Elwell points out, "Sanctifying grace renews the believer in God's image, and he experiences the moral excellence of the Lord who called him out of darkness into light."[1] Therefore, your counselees may be confident in the hope that they can celebrate the new life they have in Christ and their restored virginity! If your counselees are serious about restoring their virginity there *is* hope! They *can* be a virgin again.

JESUS IS COMING FOR HIS BRIDE THE CHURCH AND
HE EXPECTS HER TO BE A VIRGIN!
2 Corinthians 11:2

NOTES:
1. Walter A. Elwell, ed., *Evangelical Dictionary of Theology* (Grand Rapids: Baker Books, 1994), 1146.

APPENDICES

Companion Data to be used with
The Christian Counselor's Guide for Restoring Virginity
(The number of forms included in this section is limited.
Because they are designed to be used more than once with
ongoing counseling, this material *may be reproduced*
and enlarged for that purpose)

APPENDIX A

PERSONAL DATA INVENTORY

PERSONAL DATA INVENTORY

<u>IDENTIFICATION AND PERSONAL DATA</u>:

Name _____

Phone____(_____)_____

Address _____

City:_____ State:_____ Zip: _____

Occupation _____

Sex: _____ Age: _____ Birth Date: _____ Height: _____

Relationship Status: Never married___Divorced___Widowed___

Dating around _____ Engaged _____ Going Steady _____

Education (last year completed):_____ (grade)_____

Other training (list type and years) _____

_____

_____

_____

Who referred you? _____

Address _____

_____

PHYSICAL CONDITION:

What is your physician's name? _____

Address_____Phone Number: _____

Will you sign a release of information form giving us permission to contact your social worker, physician or psychiatrists/psychologist?

Yes _____ No _____

Have you lost somebody who was close to you recently? Yes ____

No ____

Please explain _____

_____

How would you describe your health (check): Very Good __Good___

Average ____

Not very well _____Other_____

How much do you weigh?_____lbs.

Have you recently had any fluctuations in your weight? Yes__No__

How much did you gain?_____How much did you lose?_____

Please provide all important illnesses, injuries or handicaps which you have now or have had in the past.

_____

_____

When was your last medical physical?_____Result: _____

_____

_____

Are you presently on any medication? Yes_____ No_____

Do you currently or have you in the past, used drugs for any other

reason other than medical purposes? Yes_____ No_____

What drug (s)?_____

_____

_____

Have you ever been severely emotional? Yes_____ No _____

If yes, please explain_____

_____

_____

Have you been arrested? Yes_____ No_____

Please explain._____

_____

Have you recently had any serious problems associated with your job, friends, business, social or other related areas of your life?

Yes_____ No _____

Please explain._____

_____

_____

RELIGIOUS BACKGROUND:

Do you believe there is a God? Yes_____ No_____ Undecided_____

Do you regard yourself as a religious person? Yes_____ No_____

Uncertain _____

Do you believe you are saved? Yes_____ No_____ Uncertain_____

Do you pray to God? No_____ Sometimes_____ Regularly_____

What denomination are you?_____ Are you a member?_____

Church Attendance per month (circle): 0 1 2 3 4 5 6 7 8

More than twice a week_____

What church did you attend in your childhood, if any? _____

_____

_____

Were you baptized as a child? Yes_____ No_____

As an adult? Yes_____ No_____

Do you read the Bible? Never____ Occasionally____ Often____

Have you undergone any changes in your religious life? Please explain.

_____

_____

PERSONALITY INSIGHT:

Have you ever undergone any counseling or psychotherapy in your

past? Yes_____ No_____

If yes, please state who your therapist or counselor was and dates seen:

_____

_____

What was the result? _____

_____

<u>Circle all of the following words that apply to you now.</u>

Persistent   Active   Nervous   Hardworking

Impatient   Excitable   Imaginative   Moody

Often-sad   Good-natured   Calm   Easily Aggravated

Lonely   Likeable   Serious   Quick-tempered

Introvert   Extrovert   Self-conscious Leader

Stodgy   Submissive   Easy going   Ambitious

Unlovable   Cautious   Self-confident Impulsive

Do it now and get it done   Do later when more convenient

<u>Sensitivity</u>:

Too sensitive_____Mildly sensitive_____Not at all sensitive_____

<u>I *like* to be held</u>:

A lot_____ Somewhat_____ Doesn't matter_____

Not very much_____ Not at all_____

I *need* to be held:

A lot_____ I like to be held_____ Doesn't matter

Not a lot_____ Not at all_____

I feel secure when I am:

Held_____ Near someone special_____

Neither when I am with someone or alone___ When I am alone___

I never thought about it___

I desire approval of the opposite sex:

A lot_____ Somewhat_____ Doesn't matter_____

Not very much_____ Not at all_____

Love is a (check all that apply):

Feeling_____ State of mind_____ Sexual act_____

Commitment_____ Emotional experience_____

I think members of the opposite sex respect me:

A lot_____ Somewhat_____ A little_____

Not very much_____ Not at all_____

<u>Fulfilling my needs are:</u>

Very important_____ Somewhat important_____

Doesn't matter_____ Not very important_____

Not important at all_____

<u>Fulfilling others' needs are:</u>

Very important_____ Somewhat important

Doesn't matter_____ Not very important_____

Not important at all_____

<u>Commitments to others are:</u>

Very important _____ Somewhat important_____

Doesn't matter_____ Not very important_____

Not important at all_____

<u>Commitments to myself are:</u>

Very important _____ Somewhat important_____

Doesn't matter_____ Not very important_____

Not important at all_____

Commitments to God are:

Very important_____ Somewhat important_____

Doesn't matter_____ Not very important_____

Not important at all_____

In what order do you place priority on your commitments?

My most important commitment is to: _____

_____

My second important commitment is to: _____

_____

My last important commitment is to: _____

_____

_____

_____

Sex draws people closer together: Yes _____ No _____
Do you think you'll lose your partner if you do not have sex?

Yes _____ No_____

If you really love someone, you should have sex with them.

True_____ False_____

Are some things too precious to lose? Yes _____ No _____

Please explain._____

_____

_____

Have you ever lost something you regretted losing? Yes_____

No_____

Please explain._____

_____

_____

What would you give or do to get it back?

Please explain._____

_____

_____

If you could change something in you life by being able to go back in time and have the opportunity to correct it, what would that be?

_____

_____

_____

How would you correct it? _____

_____

_____

<u>I believe in the following statements</u>:

There are no absolutes: Yes _____ No _____

All things are relative: Yes _____ No _____

What is truth for one person may not be for another: Yes _____

No _____

Do all religions point to the same God? Yes _____ No _____

It is all right to lie for a good reason: Yes _____ No _____

There are exceptions to everything: Yes _____ No _____

Rules are made to be broken: Yes _____ No _____

God does not want me to have any fun: Yes _____ No _____

<u>The Bible: Please check the sentence that best describes your view of Scripture.</u>

_____ Are fables and myths laced with some truth?

_____ I believe the Bible *contains* the Word of God

_____ I believe men who lived in another time and are out of touch with today wrote the Bible.

_____ I believe the Bible was written by men who were inspired by God and it is totally the Word of God.

General Observations:

Do you have insomnia? Yes _____ No _____ Sometimes _____ Are

some colors ever too bright? _____ Or seem too dull? _____

Do people sometimes look strange? Yes _____ No _____

Is it hard to distinguish faces? Yes _____ No _____

Do you sometimes have trouble judging distances? Yes ___ No ___

Do you ever hallucinate? Yes _____ No _____

Is your hearing exceptionally good or do you confuse words?

Yes _____ No _____

A yes answer to any of the above questions may indicate a medical disorder.

Have you ever been married and divorce? Yes _____ No _____

When? _____

Date of marriage _____ Your ages when married: Husband _____

Wife _____

How long did you know your spouse before marriage? _____

Length of steady dating with spouse _____

Length of Engagement _____

Please give some brief information about any other previous marriages.

_____

_____

_____

Information about children

*Check PM if child is by previous marriage.

PM_____ Name_____ Age_____Sex___Living____

Education_____ Married_____ How many years?_____

==

PM_____ Name_____ Age_____Sex___Living____

Education_____ Married_____ How many years?_____

==

PM_____ Name_____ Age_____Sex___Living____

Education_____ Married_____ How many years?_____

==

PM_____ Name_____ Age_____Sex___Living____

Education_____ Married_____ How many years?_____

==

If you were reared by anyone other than your own parents, please briefly explain.

_____

_____

_____

How many older brothers _____ sisters _____ do you have?

How many younger brothers _____ sisters _____ do you have?

BRIEFLY ANSWER THE FOLLOWING QUESTIONS:

1. What do you see is your problem?_____

_____

_____

_____

2. What have you done about it?_____

_____

_____

_____

_____

3. What can we do? (What are your expectations in coming here?)

_____

_____

_____

_____

4. As you see yourself, what kind of person are you? Describe yourself.

_____

_____

_____

_____

_____

5. What, if anything, do you fear? _____

_____

_____

_____

_____

_____

6. Is there any other information we should know? _____

_____

_____

_____

_____

_____

_____

APPENDIX B

TEMPTER-TRACKING LOG
The Temptation Tracking Form helps identify events and stimuli
that triggers and causes reoccurring sinful behavior.

TEMPTER-TRACKING LOG

DATE:_____TIME_____

SPECIFIC BEHAVIOR:

_____

_____

_____

_____

WHAT WERE YOU DOING OR WATCHING THAT TRIGGERED THE EVENT?

_____

_____

_____

_____

HOW DID YOU REACT?

_____

_____

_____

_____

WHAT DID YOU DO TO REPENT?

_____

_____

_____

_____

_____

_____

_____

RESULT:_____

_____

_____

_____

_____

_____

_____

_____

TEMPTER-TRACKING LOG

DATE:_____TIME_____

SPECIFIC BEHAVIOR:

_____

_____

_____

_____

WHAT WERE YOU DOING OR WATCHING THAT TRIGGERED THE EVENT?

_____

_____

_____

_____

HOW DID YOU REACT?

_____

_____

_____

_____

WHAT DID YOU DO TO REPENT?

_____

_____

_____

_____

_____

_____

_____

RESULT:_____

_____

_____

_____

_____

_____

_____

_____

TEMPTER-TRACKING LOG

DATE:_____TIME_____

SPECIFIC BEHAVIOR:

_____

_____

_____

_____

WHAT WERE YOU DOING OR WATCHING THAT TRIGGERED THE EVENT?

_____

_____

_____

_____

HOW DID YOU REACT?

_____

_____

_____

_____

WHAT DID YOU DO TO REPENT?

_____

_____

_____

_____

_____

_____

RESULT:_____

_____

_____

_____

_____

_____

_____

TEMPTER-TRACKING LOG

DATE:_____TIME_____

SPECIFIC BEHAVIOR:

_____

_____

_____

_____

WHAT WERE YOU DOING OR WATCHING THAT TRIGGERED THE EVENT?

_____

_____

_____

_____

HOW DID YOU REACT?

_____

_____

_____

_____

WHAT DID YOU DO TO REPENT?

_____

_____

_____

_____

_____

_____

RESULT:_____

_____

_____

_____

_____

_____

_____

TEMPTER-TRACKING LOG

DATE:_____TIME_____

SPECIFIC BEHAVIOR:

_____

_____

_____

_____

WHAT WERE YOU DOING OR WATCHING THAT TRIGGERED THE EVENT?

_____

_____

_____

_____

HOW DID YOU REACT?

_____

_____

_____

_____

WHAT DID YOU DO TO REPENT?

_____

_____

_____

_____

_____

_____

_____

RESULT:_____

_____

_____

_____

_____

_____

_____

_____

TEMPTER-TRACKING LOG

DATE:_____TIME_____

SPECIFIC BEHAVIOR:

_____

_____

_____

_____

WHAT WERE YOU DOING OR WATCHING THAT TRIGGERED THE EVENT?

_____

_____

_____

_____

HOW DID YOU REACT?

_____

_____

_____

_____

WHAT DID YOU DO TO REPENT?

_____

_____

_____

_____

_____

_____

_____

RESULT:_____

_____

_____

_____

_____

_____

_____

TEMPTER-TRACKING LOG

DATE:_____TIME_____

SPECIFIC BEHAVIOR:

_____

_____

_____

_____

WHAT WERE YOU DOING OR WATCHING THAT TRIGGERED THE EVENT?

_____

_____

_____

_____

HOW DID YOU REACT?

_____

_____

_____

_____

WHAT DID YOU DO TO REPENT?

_____

_____

_____

_____

_____

_____

_____

RESULT:_____

_____

_____

_____

_____

_____

_____

_____

APPENDIX C

HOMEWORK ASSIGNMENT FORM

Record your assignment(s) each day, including Scripture study, the time you begin, and the time you finish. Please also include comments for the insights you have gained from each study. If you need more space, you may use the back of the page.

HOMEWORK ASSIGNMENT FORM

SUNDAY

NAME:_____Date_____

START TIME_____ FINISH TIME_____

SCRIPTURE(S) _____

_____

_____

_____

HOW DOES THIS APPLY TO MY LIFE?

_____

_____

_____

_____

HAVE YOU APPLIED THIS TO YOUR LIFE TODAY? WHAT INSIGHTS HAVE YOU GAINED?

_____

_____

_____

_____

_____

_____

_____

_____

_____

_____

_____

_____

_____

_____

_____

_____

_____

_____

_____

_____

_____

_____

_____

HOMEWORK ASSIGNMENT FORM

MONDAY

NAME:_____Date_____

START TIME_____ FINISH TIME_____

SCRIPTURE(S) _____

_____

_____

_____

HOW DOES THIS APPLY TO MY LIFE?

_____

_____

_____

_____

HAVE YOU APPLIED THIS TO YOUR LIFE TODAY? WHAT INSIGHTS HAVE YOU GAINED?

_____

_____

_____

_____

_____

_____

_____

_____

_____

_____

_____

_____

_____

_____

_____

_____

_____

_____

_____

_____

_____

HOMEWORK ASSIGNMENT FORM

TUESDAY

NAME:_____Date_____

 START TIME_____ FINISH TIME_____

SCRIPTURE(S) _____

_____

_____

_____

HOW DOES THIS APPLY TO MY LIFE?

_____

_____

_____

_____

HAVE YOU APPLIED THIS TO YOUR LIFE TODAY? WHAT INSIGHTS HAVE YOU GAINED?

_____

_____

_____

HOMEWORK ASSIGNMENT FORM

WEDNESDAY

NAME:_____Date_____

 START TIME_____ FINISH TIME_____

SCRIPTURE(S) _____

_____

_____

_____

HOW DOES THIS APPLY TO MY LIFE?

_____

_____

_____

_____

HAVE YOU APPLIED THIS TO YOUR LIFE TODAY? WHAT INSIGHTS HAVE YOU GAINED?

_____

_____

_____

HOMEWORK ASSIGNMENT FORM

THURSDAY

NAME:_____Date_____

START TIME_____ FINISH TIME_____

SCRIPTURE(S) _____

_____

_____

_____

HOW DOES THIS APPLY TO MY LIFE?

_____

_____

_____

_____

HAVE YOU APPLIED THIS TO YOUR LIFE TODAY? WHAT INSIGHTS HAVE YOU GAINED?

_____

_____

_____

_____

_____

_____

_____

_____

_____

_____

_____

_____

_____

_____

_____

_____

_____

_____

_____

_____

HOMEWORK ASSIGNMENT FORM

FRIDAY

NAME:_____Date_____

 START TIME_____ FINISH TIME_____

SCRIPTURE(S) _____

_____

_____

_____

HOW DOES THIS APPLY TO MY LIFE?

_____

_____

_____

_____

HAVE YOU APPLIED THIS TO YOUR LIFE TODAY? WHAT
INSIGHTS HAVE YOU GAINED?

_____

_____

_____

HOMEWORK ASSIGNMENT FORM

SATURDAY

NAME:_____Date_____

START TIME_____ FINISH TIME_____

SCRIPTURE(S) _____

_____

_____

_____

HOW DOES THIS APPLY TO MY LIFE?

_____

_____

_____

_____

HAVE YOU APPLIED THIS TO YOUR LIFE TODAY? WHAT INSIGHTS HAVE YOU GAINED?

_____

_____

_____

_____

_____

_____

_____

_____

_____

_____

_____

_____

_____

_____

_____

_____

_____

_____

_____

_____

_____

_____

BIBLIOGRAPHY

Adams, Jay E., *The Christian Counselor's Manual* (Grand Rapids: Zondervan Publishing   House 1973).

___ *Marriage, Divorce, and Remarriage in the Bible* (Grand Rapids: Zondervan Publishing House, 1980).

Almy, Gary and Carol Tharp Alma with Jerry Jenkins, *Addicted to Recovery* (Eugene: Harvest House Publ., 1994).

Anderson, Kerby, B.S., M.A., M.F.S., "Kerby Anderson's Commentaries." http://www.probe.org/docs/c-divorce.html. 12 January, 2000.

Associated Press, "Dirty song lyrics can prompt early teen sex. Degrading messages influence sexual behavior, study finds." http://msnbc.msn.com/id/14227775/?GT1=8404 (7 August, 2006.

Ayer, Eleanor, *It's Okay to Say No: Choosing Sexual Abstinence* (New York: The Rosen Publishing Group, Inc., —).

Barna, George, *The Future of the American Family* (Chicago: Moody Press, 1993).

Barnhart, Clarence L., ed., *The American College Encyclopedic Dictionary* (Chicago: Spencer Press, Inc., 1959).

Bunyan, John, *The Pilgrim's Progress* (Edinburgh: The Banner of Truth Trust, 1977).

CNN's *Talkback Live*, "Mike Long." 3 January, 2001.

CNN's *Talkback Live,* "Ester Drill." 3 January, 2001.

Costello, Robert B., Editor-in-Chief, *Random House Webster's College Dictionary* (New York: Random House, 1990).

Elliot, Elisabeth, *Passion and Purity: Learning to Bring Your Love under Christ's Control* (Grand Rapids: Fleming H. Revell, 1984).

Elwell, Walter A., ed., *Evangelical Dictionary of Theology* (Grand Rapids: Baker Books, 1994).

Evert, Jason, *If You Really Loved Me* (El Cajon: Catholic Answers Inc., 2003).

Franklin Bookman Electronic *King James Bible*, Version 770.

Geisler, Normal L. Baker, *Encyclopedia of Christian Apologetic* (Grand Rapids: Baker Books, 1999).

Hayford, Jack W., Litt.d., General Editor., *Spirit Filled Life Bible* |NIV| (Nashville: Thomas Nelson Publishers, 1991).

Indianapolis Star (Indianapolis), 8 March 2001.

Is Sex Safe? A Look at: Sexually Transmitted Diseases (Lewiston: Life Cycle Books, 1998).

Keroack, Eric J, M.D., FACOG and Dr. John R. Diggs Jr., M.D., "Bonding Imperative," A Special Report from the Abstinence Medical Council. As quoted by Abstinence Clearinghouse, 30 April 2001.

Lipman, Eugene J., trans., The *Mishnah* (Toronto: George J. McLeod Limited, 1970).

McIlkhaney Jr., Joe. S., *Why Condoms Aren't Safe* (Colorado Springs: Focus on the Family, 1994).

"Neural Oxytocinegric systems as Genomic Targets for Hormones and as Modulators of Hormone-Dependent Behaviors," Rockefeller University NY, 1999.

Poor, Henry V., Advisory Editor., *You and the Law* (Pleasantville: Reader's Digest, 1977).

Research Alert, *Future Vision* (Naperville, Ill.: Sourcebooks Trade, 1991).

Talkback Live, "Mike Long." Produced by: Cable Network News, January 3, 2001.

Talkback Live, "Esther Drill." Produced by: Cable Network News, January 3, 2001.

Teachman, J.D., J. Thomas, and K. Paasch, "Legal Status and the Stability of Coresidential Unions," *Demography*, November 1991, 571-83. As quoted in *Good News About Sex and Marriage*, p. 71.

The 700 Club, "Andy Pettitte." Produced by The Christian Broadcasting Network, July 18, 2005.

The 700 Club, "Jason Illian." Produced by The Christian Broadcasting Network, July 19, 2005.

Thomas, Gary, *Where True Love Waits: Sexual Abstinence Programs* (Christianity Today, 1999).

Thompson, Sharon, *Going All the Way* (New York: Hill and Wang, 1995).

Vine, W.E., M.A., *Vine's Expository Dictionary of New Testament Words: A Comprehensive Dictionary of the Original Greek Words with their Precise Meanings for English Readers* (Mc Lean: Mac Donald Publishing Company, ——).

Wells, David F., *Losing Our Virtue* (Grand Rapids: William B. Eerdmans Publishing Company, 1998).

Wheat, M.D., ed., and Gaye Wheat, *Intended for Pleasure, 3rd Edition* (Grand Rapids: Fleming H. Revell, 2001).

Wilson, P.B., *Knight in Shining Armor* (Eugene: Harvest House Publishers, 1995).

The Father and Daughter
Writing Team of
J.P. Sloane and Shannon Sloane

J.P. Sloane

J.P. has always enjoyed researching the diversity of the Christian faith. In that pursuit, he has availed himself of educational opportunities at the following schools from which he graduated: the Institute of Charismatic Studies, Oral Roberts University, Moody Bible Institute, and The Institute of Jewish-Christian Studies. J.P. also earned a B.A., *Summa Cum Laude*, from The Master's College where he also studied at the IBEX campus in Israel. While at the Master's College he worked on his M.A. in Biblical Counseling. J.P. is currently working on a Doctorate at Trinity Theological Seminary.

Through the years, J.P. has appeared on such Christian television programs as *The 700 Club, Lester Sumrall Today*, *Richard Roberts Live*, LaSea Broadcasting's *World Harvest*, and Trinity Broadcasting Network's *Praise the Lord*, to mention a few.

J.P. currently appears in Marquis "Who's Who in the World" and "Who's Who in America." He is also featured in the "2000 Outstanding Intellectuals of the 21st Century" and the "Dictionary of International Biography" (Cambridge, England).

Shannon Sloane

Shannon Sloane is a graduate of Oral Roberts University in Tulsa, Oklahoma, with a Bachelor of Science in Communication Arts and a minor in Journalism and holds a Master's Degree in Biblical Counseling from The Master's College in Los Angeles, California.

Shannon is a former Miss San Diego Supreme Beauty. At age nine, she began working in television and radio commercials. When she was a high school senior, she co-hosted a Christian radio program on WCFY. As Director for a *Crisis Pregnancy Center,* Shannon counseled hundreds of young women and girls. Relying on the Bible, Shannon developed a unique biblical insight and love for troubled young women.

Many people, in over 47 countries, remember Shannon as the "Dove Girl" on the internationally televised Gospel Music Association's *Dove Awards.*

As a labor of love to fight the lies of Satan and the world, Shannon teamed up with her father to write this unique and encouraging biblically-based Christian counselor's volume and its companion edition, *You Can Be a Virgin Again.* Shannon and her father are convinced that a person *can* recapture their innocence and virginity through God if they truly have a desire. Together, they bring a unique biblically-based insight on God's promise of restoration.